Rigged Money

Rigged Money

BEATING WALL STREET AT ITS OWN GAME

Lee Munson

WILEY

John Wiley & Sons, Inc.

Published by John Wiley & Sons, Inc., Hoboken, New Jersey.
Published simultaneously in Canada.

For general information on our other products and services or for technical support,
please contact our Customer Care Department within the United States at (800)
762-2974, outside the United States at (317) 572-3993, or fax (317) 572-4002.

Wiley also publishes its books in a variety of electronic formats. Some content that
appears in print may not be available in electronic books. For more information
about Wiley products, visit our web site at www.wiley.com.

Library of Congress Cataloging-in-Publication Data:

Munson, Lee.
    Rigged money : beating Wall Street at its own game / Lee Munson.
        p. cm.
    Includes index.
    ISBN 978-1-118-09968-1 (cloth); ISBN 978-1-118-17112-7 (ebk);
    ISBN 978-1-118-17113-4 (ebk); ISBN 978-1-118-17114-1 (ebk)
        1. Investments.   2. Wall Street (New York, N.Y.)   I. Title.
    HG4515.M865 2012
    332.6–dc23

                                                    2011029146

Printed in the United States of America
10 9 8 7 6 5 4 3 2 1

*To my wife and daughter, for allowing
me to follow my passion.*

Contents

Preface

Did it really take the 2008 meltdown to clue in the population that Wall Street was somehow rigged? Don't be naïve. For 400 years, common stock and the trading of it has never been designed to make or lose you money. It's simply designed for you to participate. Most people ask the wrong questions either out of a lack of understanding of the game or because Wall Street, like a hypnotist, is suggesting the question. This book is written to unravel and illuminate those questions. I get to the bottom of why it's necessary for Wall Street to have a strategy for every investor, a market for every man, and a philosophy to suit any temperament. If you are a buy and hold investor and are disillusioned by the meltdown, or if you found your asset allocation pie chart to be dubious at best, keep reading. I show you where those concepts came from, why they work or don't work, and let you be the judge. The very first company that ever floated stock in 1602 was a shaky operation that paid its dividend half in cash and half in spice. Not exactly awe inspiring. That is the start of the rigged system.

You only need to make one decision right here and right now. Do you want to be successful? If you are a young investor, you need to learn how to rub your two pennies together so that you can create a nest egg for when you may not be able to work for money. If you've spent a lifetime saving, you need to understand how to turn that nest egg into a cash-flow machine to provide yourself a lifetime of income without having to be productive in terms of our capitalist system. How is it that people are going to be retired for 30 years and not work? One hundred years ago, retirement was a euphemism for dying.

Everyone must engage the system. If you're lucky enough to have a great pension, where do you think that money comes from? The system. Do you understand what a pension manager has to do to make a check appear in your mailbox every month? We live in a global society in which industry and job security from here on out are questionable. It's not enough to preserve your capital when you quit working if you want to keep up the lifestyle you're accustomed to.

All you have to do is take one action: read this book. I don't give you all the answers, but I will tell you how to prevent Wall Street from getting you off track. Learn how Wall Street gives you answers to questions that you didn't ask.

Why Did I Write This Book?

April 1, 2001: An article was published on that April Fools' Day by the *New York Observer*. The guy who sat next to me at Bear Stearns had a buddy named George Gurley. I had hung out with George mostly drinking with a group of guys for a few months before he asked me if I wanted to do an article with him describing the crazy world of Wall Street. It was never my intention to have my name in it, but as a wiser person today, I should have known better.

George invited me out drinking one night, started a tab, and we hung out. There were several sessions in which I espoused my philosophy about Wall Street, how it worked, how it was rigged, and the over-the-top lifestyle that people lived during a market top. I said all those words and I meant all those words. My only lapse in judgment was drinking too much as George served more and more pints of beer. I could have been more tactful in delivering my ideas, and George Gurley could have been a more professional journalist rather than encouraging me into a night of drinking to extract vulgar language over substance. In the end we were both products of the excessive times. Times have changed. I said more than 10 years ago that New York was burning and that it would fall. Five months later it did—for real. After the planes hit the Twin Towers, my fate was sealed. I would move before the end of the year back to New Mexico.

From there I got a great job at Charles Schwab, at the time the most wholesome place to work on Wall Street. It gave new meaning to squeaky-clean. And yes, I found it telling that they would take me with all the negative public relations that came with that article just because they simply wanted my experience. It also gave me a shot at maturity. This Fortune 500 company saw more than just a guy who could make money. They saw me as somebody who could do good things for Wall Street and Main Street. I began studying, first for the Certified Financial Planning designation and then to earn a Chartered Financial Analyst charter. I bought my first home and had my first child, a daughter. Will I ever be able to explain my lapse in judgment to her?

I want to teach my daughter that even if certain people in society disagree with you or what you do—follow your passion. You respect the fact that some people are ignorant and will never approve. In essence, I want to tell her: don't apologize and don't back down.

Now that I'm older, I like what *Business Insider* did without contacting me in publishing a 10-year flashback of the ordeal. That was the defining moment because it reminded me of something. It reminded me of what I was trying to tell people back in 2001. The *Business Insider* retrospective of the article that came out April 1, 2011, reminded me of one thing: I had the idea in the first place, but I needed a way to communicate it to a wider audience with more wisdom and preferably with less profanity and offensive metaphors.

Why did I start the firm? Because eventually I felt that my previous firm wasn't the wholesome place it used to be. It wasn't being run by the same CEO anymore, and I didn't feel intellectually honest about what I was doing. But honestly I just wanted to do it my way. Isn't that the American dream? It was Chuck Schwab's. And that's why I started Portfolio, LLC in 2008. I wanted to represent clients only and I wanted to not have a gag rule. I wanted to have the ability to politely or otherwise tell people how things worked, expose it, and make my clients money doing it.

Who Is This Book For?

I'm not here to shock you anymore. The ideas in the book are jarring enough. The substance of what I have to say here is outrageous. This book is for people who want to grow their money, protect their assets, and instinctively know that there is a house out there stacking the odds against them. I'm part of the house because I'm a Wall Street operator. But I'm also hired by my clients to only work in their best interests and to get them the results that they request. I only serve one master: my clients. And that includes you, the reader. Whether you're starting off, have been investing for 50 years, or are a professional investor yourself, this book is designed to free your mind and to act as a starting point for your financial education.

This is for people who want to reset their perception by getting rid of a lot of misperceptions. In this book I talk about a lot of different things—some positive and some negative. There is no clear-cut way to do things, and if anything, you'll see the upside and downside of both arguments even if I clearly have a bias. The most important thing the reader can do after finishing this book is to go back and read the original sources which you can find at the end of this book. As a student of St. John's College, the third oldest institution in this country, we were taught to read only the original text. These words are my original text. If you want to go further in your education of how the game works, you need to read what I read. St. John's taught me how to read! It was the single most important contributing factor to my ability to think and consistently refer back to the original texts. I'm not challenging anybody's work. I just have my own ideas. Most people I've known in the business quote books that they've never read and use ideas that they have never critically thought through. Given the education I received at St. John's, I find that unacceptable.

What's in the Book?

I break up the book into three sections: Part One Old School . . . Of Thought, Part Two Wall Street: The Set Up, and Part Three Surviving the Rigged Game. Old school is just that—ideas that are past their prime. But is it that simple? The very idea of buying and holding something for a long period of time seems reckless and without any real thought. I look at two different companies, the very first was publicly traded, and one of the best performing of the last 40 years. You would think the incredible returns would prove a buy-and-hold approach. Hindsight identifies a needle in a haystack. But it doesn't help you today going forward. Buy and hold is a phrase that has very little actual meaning and doesn't describe any type of investment philosophy as much as a dogma or sales pitch. Even worse, as we enter the modern age of the asset-allocation pie chart, we realize risk has been understated and the very nature of illustration has been misrepresented. Many salespeople in my industry find these ideas dangerous. Why? Essentially, I indict their intellectual credibility and expose their deficiencies. By the end of this section you'll have a clear idea of how to move forward without the baggage that you and Wall Street have saddled each other with.

Once we understand risk and how that idea has over the years been misrepresented by Wall Street, what other structural changes in the business have contributed to the delinquency of investors? In Part Two, we go back to the year I was born. Through several key rules set forth by the U.S. Congress, the unintended consequences include devaluing the credibility of stock research and taking away the choice of the American worker to engage or not engage the stock market. By creating competition and lowering prices, we ended up becoming cynical and distrusting of the market structure itself. Cheap discount commissions, 401(k)s, and electronic trading were all supposed to help us in some way, but it doesn't feel that way. I'm going to help you understand why you should care. We want to look past the problems and understand how to turn it into your advantage.

In order to survive the rigged game, you have to control how the other side sees you. In Part Three, I will give you a few examples of how far off the mark Wall Street's perception of you can be. From there, we'll look at a few popular investment ideas. Why are exchange traded funds (ETFs) popular? And what should you do with them? Is gold a bubble? Money? Or is it just another way for Wall Street to get a commission? For intrepid investors, I offer my version of trading options. If old and stodgy is your style, sit back for Chapter 11, where I explain why dividends matter and why on some level they're irrelevant. Most importantly, I will tell you how all these things get turned into a pitch which Wall Street cares about nothing except selling you something. To top it off, I unveil the New Scam. Thanks to deregulation and a complete disregard for moral hazard, we start a new century with banking and brokerage joined together like it was 100 years ago, with essentially the same effect: bedlam. Ladies and gentlemen, I give you the rigged game!

Additional Materials

For updates and more information, go to www.riggedmoney.com.

Acknowledgments

I'd like to thank acquisition editor Laura Walsh for her passion behind the project and Judy Howarth for putting up with my writing. I want to acknowledge my incredible luck of having Jonathan Gake show up on my doorstep and wanting to work for me. Without him the manuscript would still be in my mind. Lorraine Ell for her constant eye on detail and everybody at Portfolio who put up with my days of absence in order to write the book. Needless to say, my wife and daughter made significant sacrifices and I want to acknowledge that I will be spending more time at home after this book is published.

But what about those who made it possible to write the book on a bigger scale? First and foremost, thank you to Stephen Schwartz, Mark Ronda, and the crew at Prime Charter in the late 1990s. I could not have asked for a better place to spend my first four years in the business.

I want to thank the management at Bear Stearns for realizing we were a bad fit right off the bat. It couldn't have happened to a better batch of people. I also want to thank all of the producers at CNBC who gave me a shot to be myself and coached me along the way, especially Dan Holland. Special thanks to Larry Kudlow for teaching me to grab hold of my idea and not let go.

PART

I

OLD SCHOOL . . . OF THOUGHT

CHAPTER 1

Buy and Hope: The Scam?

Over the years there has always been a debate over whether investors should buy and hold stocks and never sell them versus the active pursuit of trading stocks to earn profits. I have no idea why anyone would take the risk that a corporation will last longer than you will or for that matter what buy and hold means. Why would anyone purchase a stock, and then never sell it? One common reason is that if the stock pays a dividend—the earnings of a corporation paid out to its shareholders—you can get cash flow just for holding the shares. Some people just want to accumulate wealth and hold onto stocks forever, but even the desire for endless fortune doesn't mean an endless holding period. Would you still want to own shares of a typewriter company?

Of course the basic assumption of buying and holding a stock is a better bet than the old adage of buy low sell high. The concept we are exploring here is buy and never sell. Who would want to sell a company that is supposed to make profits over the long haul? Plus, how would you know when to sell? If you hold a stock forever, it shouldn't matter when you buy it since it will be a one-time transaction. This would be fine if most corporations made money in large amounts forever and paid out the profits to you. If you suffered the horror of a basic finance class in college, the value of a company was determined by looking at the long-term earnings or cash flow of a firm if you wanted to answer the test questions correctly. That would be fine if the world had no shares traded on public exchanges where the price to buy and sell is determined each day by supply and demand, not rational analysis of a firm's true value. Plus, I have no idea how people in a public market would ever come to a consensus to figure out the value of a big company like General Electric (GE). Even the executives at GE can't tell you the real value of the company. This is because there is no real value, only the price a buyer and seller can agree on at that moment in time in which the stock trades hands.

Holding a stock has to have some purpose to the buyer. Is the collection of dividends over time the motivating factor? What if the company stops paying dividends, do you continue to hold the stock? We could spend a lot of time discussing the matter, but buy and hold is simply an observation of what one does, not a strategy. If you owned stock in Philip Morris and held it for 50 years, people would have told you your stock was doomed to fail in light of the company's continuous legal litigation. In fact, it was one of the best performing stocks of the last 50 years, but you would have had to hold it a long time against the best advice of experts. On the other hand, you could have gone with the crowd and purchased stock in a good old-fashioned company that made a product that wasn't going to go away. You could have bought stock in General Motors, only to have your investment go belly up in the recent financial crisis. Nobody back in the 1950s could predict what would be around today, nor should we try to make guesses about how the world will be in 50 years. Let's leave that to shows like NOVA or to Hollywood. It's more fun and cool to watch years later when we see how far off we were. The question is not whether to buy and hold. By getting you to ask if you should buy and hold, Wall Street has tricked you into thinking about it as if it is a strategy. No reasonable person would bet that anything is a sure thing for 50 years, so we need to start off with the first insight on Wall Street: Buy and hold is dead. But the truth is, it never really existed.

I think the first person to say this was a stockbroker. Wall Street manufactures publicly traded securities for people to consume. Some work, most don't. Do you want someone to buy a product from your store only to have it returned? No. So why would you think Wall Street would ever want their goods returned? Sure, money is made when people buy and sell shares, but they never end up back on the same shelf they came from.

We will all die sometime, and the desire to make money during our lifetime is just human nature. Why not accept this fact and move on? Wall Street knows this is how people feel, and they provide the public with limitless ways to engage the markets. The problem is that each idea is presented as if there is only one solution to choose. Think about it; everyone is looking to make easy money. If you had "the answer," why would you need to look anywhere else? That is what this buy-and-hold thing is all about. You make a smart decision one day and never look back. Many people, especially after the dot-com crash, and definitely after the 2008 financial crisis, found out that buy and hold was not a successful strategy. And there are other similar scams that resemble this perennial idea. I use the term scam not in the sense that something doesn't work, but that it is presented as the eternal system. You can't beat the system unless you know the game.

Blame the Dutch!

Forget blaming the French for socialism or Wall Street fat cats for financial meltdowns. It was the Dutch that got us into this mess more than 400 years ago. While trade and commerce is an ancient practice, the first stock didn't spontaneously generate until 1602, when the Dutch East India Company was founded. Why was this important, outside of being the first stock? First of all, this was the first *joint-stock* company, meaning regular people like middle class merchants were able to invest in a public company. On September 1 the public subscription period was over. Five hundred thirty-eight subscribers, including craftsmen and small entrepreneurs, were given shares that were freely transferable.[1] Before this there was a barrier to entry for investments. The idea of selling a piece of a company in order to lower the risk to any one person was not new, but allowing anybody with the money to buy shares was ground breaking. The Amsterdam Stock Exchange was established the same year just so people could trade shares of this new corporation.

Why did it take so long for the madness to start? First off, you can't sell stock to those that have no money, freedom, or laws protecting ownership. The feudal system of a Lord owning the land and you working on it doesn't cut it. Starting around 1433 the Duke of Burgundy, having won the genetic lottery, decided to unite towns previously under no rule into a cohesive sovereign nation. Amsterdam was one of those towns that became quite wealthy as the shipping business with Asia boomed. Despite a war with Spain that lasted 80 years and independence that wasn't official until 1648, the Dutch Republic managed to become one of the first free economies. It worked. While Portugal and Spain were used to the limelight of international trade, they lacked property rights and contractual obligations. Remember that the Dutch were a republic, and while there was not the same personal freedoms we think of today, not having to deal with monarchs who held ultimate power was good for business. It was this ability to make contracts with laws and enforce them that allowed corporations to open up to the general population of wealthy merchants. In the end it was the rule of law that gave rise to what we think of as economic freedom. It helped that the Dutch had one of the strongest navies in Europe at the time. When the Dutch East India Company started to take control of East Asian trading routes, it was met with strong opposition from Portugal and England.

While this is all very interesting, how did the stock do? Investors received an average 25 percent return on their money during the first 15 years.[2] Eventually creating monopolies, the company dominated trade with Asia and at one point paid out a 40 percent dividend to shareholders.[3] Does this sound like a stock you would like to own? With a return so rich and dividends paying you to stick with it, nobody would look this gift horse in the mouth. This was the first buy-and-hold stock—no hope needed. At the peak, the company even had 40 warships and 10,000 soldiers on the payroll to keep market share. At the time I guess people were not worried about socially conscious investing. Also, it wasn't just great management or a business idea that helped its track record. For the first 21 years the company had a monopoly from the government on colonialism. It took a few years for operations to become profitable enough to pay a dividend, starting in 1610. After priming the pump with a government monopoly and borrowed money it was not hard for a whopping 18 percent average annual dividend to be paid for most of the 200 years it was around.

So, what happened to the first great and powerful multinational corporation? After almost 200 years of making money for shareholders, inefficiencies and corruption sank the ship. The industry was changing and the ability of the firm to keep up was challenged. While many reasons are given, the one I find most fascinating was the dividend policy. Starting around 1730, the dividends paid by the company exceeded the *earnings*.

earnings   An actual profit, the fundamental point of capitalism, and a key pressure point between shareholders and corporate management. When earnings exist, shareholders generally tend to nag companies to share the wealth. After all, shareholders by definition have a claim on earnings. However, just because earnings exist doesn't mean you will get your hands on them. In some cases, the desire for management to pay and shareholders to receive earnings are so strong, dividends are paid out without actual earnings to cover it. This is called denial. Generally denial ends in bankruptcy.

Only by borrowing money short term against future income was the company able to continue. (This sounds a lot like companies that go out of business today.) Nationalized in 1796 and officially shut down in 1800, the company left shareholders with nothing in the end. Sure, if you had put money down in 1602 and never sold there were no complaints, but by 1800 you would be on the sixth generation of stockholders. Your great- great- great- grandkid would not be happy. Obviously, despite the loss of value in the end the company was a huge success. You can see why investors would spend the next 400 years trying to find the next Dutch East India Company. All your family would need to do is establish a legacy of wealth.

The bottom line is the system worked out well. It was the beginning of convincing the uneducated public to put up money to capitalize a shaky operation and strip out the value using borrowed money until the entire organization fell apart. Paying a dividend kept investors holding onto shares, at least until the dividend became a liability that eroded the assets and blew up the company. Democratizing wealth for those that took the risk was here to stay.

All the Wrong Moves?

As we learned from the Dutch East India Company, a long-term track record of good investor returns doesn't ensure success over the long haul. So, if one of the most successful companies in history can go bust, what about the worst companies? What if a company was in a constant state of being sued, sold a product that killed people, and had a rich dividend payout that was anything but safe? Just to be clear, my father is a lung cancer survivor. He smoked for most of his life until the day he was diagnosed. At our firm, I recently made the decision to not invest money in tobacco companies. This was easy to do and I don't have a strong opinion about it, but when there are thousands of companies to invest in, why worry about a client who may be offended by it? Also, I find that people who are okay buying tobacco companies can change their minds when a loved one is affected. Now that I have disclosed my biases, let's let the numbers speak.

People hate tobacco companies, and Philip Morris is the biggest around. While smoking may not be great for your health, a portfolio that had the advantage of a crystal ball would have profited from investing in Philip Morris. It was not always the big dog of death. Back in the 1960s the firm was the underdog until the Marlboro Man took pole position and led the company to cigarette heaven in 1983. Think about it: You are an investor looking at buying the sixth largest cigarette company back in 1960. Would you be thinking to yourself that this is a great long-term investment? What about buying the leader, or at least the top three? Twenty-three years later it would be number one, but only because it changed the way it operated along the way. You would have known none of this back then. Believing that management would pull through over decades of adversity would require ignorance or a leap of faith. How could you have known that the tobacco giants would be sued by states and a slew of people? But to make an investment that they would lose and rise again would be wishful thinking. It happened over and over again.

Investors don't like when the government sues their companies. Share prices tend to go down if you can't figure out the future liability of a lawsuit. When the aim of suing the company is to put it out of business, or effectively damage it permanently, shareholders tend to exit. So, with the tobacco companies being sued all the time, why would you want to take the risk? For starters, tobacco companies didn't lose cases until their luck ran out in the 1990s when individual states ganged up and filed the largest suit in the industry. It was called the Tobacco Master Settlement Agreement (MSA). In 1998, 46 states settled for a total of $206 billion over the course of the 25-year agreement. Of course, the irony is that the companies will have to stay in business in order for the states to collect. With balancing state budgets a problem these days, the profitability of tobacco firms is important to the very states that sued them. In fact, there is a vested interest in keeping tobacco companies alive so states can continue to get money out of them.

While this is not only socially horrible and expensive, the reality of the returns tells a different story. Between 1925 and 2003, the company earned an average compound return of 17 percent, while the S&P 500 returned 9.3 percent during the same period of time.[4] Every time it was sued, Philip Morris' stock price would hit the bricks only to rebound to higher levels. I remember the first time I played with the evil empire when I was a stockbroker still in my 20s. It was around the time of the 1998 settlement, and I watched the firm trade lower and lower. A broker friend of mine said his friend was an attorney and studied the case. The attorney was convinced the MSA would kill Philip Morris. There was only one observation I made: The stock was still trading and states needed the money. As the dot-com crash killed the economy, the share price of Philip Morris fell in kind. In the low 20s, the dividend was close to 9 percent. I wasn't a stock genius, but knew that investors would come in to buy the shares like they always did now that the dividend was rich and your other option was losing your shirt in tech stocks. The money flowed into the stock as *fundamentals*, a high yield, and the cynical investing public saw the opportunity and took it. It wasn't great for society, but neither were the colonial activities of the Dutch East India Company. Plus, a stock doesn't know you own it.

The effect was making money, and my clients were happy. A healthy dividend yield allowed those that wanted to take on the risk of further bad news to earn an above market return for sticking around. Keep in mind though that these were massive lawsuits that could have destroyed the companies. If you were a buy-and-hope investor in Philip Morris, you had to keep it together while you watched your investment take a nosedive, sometimes more than 50 percent, when the lawsuits started to heat up. To compensate you for this volatility, Philip Morris raised its prices and continued to pay shareholders a large part of the profit in the form of dividends.

fundamentals   Also called "funny-mentals," referring to the analysis of the actual business as opposed to the stock price, stock chart, or hot tip found on the Internet. Fundamentalists, those who invest based on fundamentals, will go on and on about how their company is great and profitable in response to why the stock price fails to go up. Their counterparts, simply known as "mental," will suggest a hot stock needs no profits, which explains how a stock grows into a bubble.

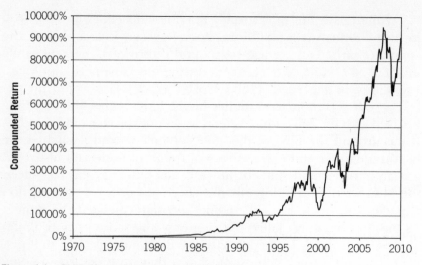

Figure 1.1   Philip Morris Performance 1970–2010

In turn shareholders had to have the guts to reinvest those cash dividends and buy more Philip Morris. This is the rub. That compounded 17 percent return was only achieved if you reinvested the dividends each quarter (Figure 1.1). Is it reasonable that you might have been tempted to take the money and run? If you did you missed out. My point is simple. It is hard to think through how history will be written, and long-term investing finds success in unusual places.

So, how did they really do it? Philip Morris started to diversify the profits not paid out in rich dividends to buy up food companies. This should have been obvious, as the company was simply buying more things people used every day. Turning the company into a conglomerate allowed Philip Morris to diversify its holdings, lower its risk, and increase returns to shareholders. At least that was the idea. In 1988 Philip Morris acquired Kraft and became the largest cheese maker on earth (Figure 1.2). By 2007 Kraft was spun off as a separate company. This was but one acquisition that Philip Morris made over the years, but gives you an idea of the buying and selling of other assets that contributed to the outsized returns of the firm.

While the domestic tobacco business is dying off, literally, we export our cancer internationally to keep up profits. In 2008 Philip Morris, which changed its name to Altria Group in 2003, spun off Philip Morris International. Notice they kept the name for the foreign

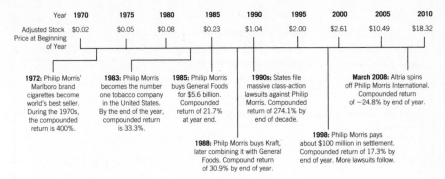

Year	1970	1975	1980	1985	1990	1995	2000	2005	2010
Adjusted Stock Price at Beginning of Year	$0.02	$0.05	$0.08	$0.23	$1.04	$2.00	$2.61	$10.49	$18.32

1972: Philip Morris' Marlboro brand cigarettes become world's best seller. During the 1970s, the compounded return is 400%.

1983: Philip Morris becomes the number one tobacco company in the United States. By the end of the year, compounded return is 33.3%.

1985: Philip Morris buys General Foods for $5.6 billion. Compounded return of 21.7% at year end.

1990s: States file massive class-action lawsuits against Philip Morris. Compounded return of 274.1% by end of decade.

March 2008: Altria spins off Philip Morris International. Compounded return of −24.8% by end of year.

1988: Philip Morris buys Kraft, later combining it with General Foods. Compound return of 30.9% by end of year.

1998: Philip Morris pays about $100 million in settlement. Compounded return of 17.3% by end of year. More lawsuits follow.

Figure 1.2   Philip Morris Timeline 1970–2010

population. I guess there is still a strong demand for the Marlboro Man abroad. In the end perhaps you could have seen all along that Americans would keep smoking, profits would be diversified into cheese makers, and states would be given incentives to keep Philip Morris alive to pay off billion-dollar settlements. All of this would end with the idea that our glamorized culture of smoking would have appeal to emerging economies as they earned enough money to buy a pack of reds. This is just not the bet I want to try and figure out.

Disneyland Adventure Kills Wall Street

Everyone needs a little fantasy to escape the day-to-day grind. In my profession, finance professors love to offer high-minded examples of what-if scenarios in order to prove their pet theory at the time. One of the classic examples is taking a select group of stocks and reinvesting the dividends over time in order to show amazing results for a buy-and-hold strategy. Not to worry, when the stock market hits the wall, the same examples are given with U.S. Treasury bonds showing how they would have done better during a specific period of time. Let's have some fun.

It's 1970 and you decide to take the kids to Disneyland. The place is packed and the stock market is coming off the highs of the last year. During the 1960s the stock market did fairly well, more than doubling in the last decade, but in 1969 it was down 8.5 percent. Today you will take the pulse of the American consumer and look for companies that are ripe for buying. This is a long-term investment project, so you are not worried that 1974 will wipe all of your profits out. Hey, you can't predict the future.

(Continued)

First off you buy tickets to the Magic Kingdom, which are not cheap. After paying the piper the kids want a Coca-Cola, which has a soda monopoly inside the park. Your kids immediately hop on Mission to Mars that utilizes computer technology by IBM. During the ride you sit outside and have a smoke break, lighting up a Marlboro made by Philip Morris. Once the kids get out, Mickey Mouse appears and a camera using Kodak film captures the precious memory.

After getting back home, with what little money you have left, you decide to purchase these five stocks and hold them because this is the *future* (and so can you!). And because you were in the Magic Kingdom, you somehow manage to invest all of your dividends and don't have to pay any tax on them, mainly due to pixie dust provided by Tinker Bell. Let's look at how the fantasy works out.

1970–2010 Results

After visiting Disneyland in 1970 with your children, you divide your remaining $100 evenly among five stocks, investing $20 in each one (Table 1.1). You do the math and call your broker on January 2, telling him you want to buy 35.71 shares of Disney, 2.74 shares of Eastman Kodak, 3.42 shares of IBM, 37.04 shares of Coca-Cola, and 1,000 shares of Philip Morris. (It's a magical world, so you're able to buy a fraction of a share.) Your broker's a really nice guy so he doesn't charge you any commissions for this trade, although in the real world you would have had to pay him a commission. You also discover that you can reinvest your dividends without paying taxes. "Groovy," you say to yourself as you enter a magical investing fantasy.

Table 1.1   Number of Shares Purchased on 1/2/1970 (Adjusted Closing Prices)

	Disney	Eastman Kodak	IBM	Coca-Cola	Philip Morris	S&P 500*
Invest	$20.00	$20.00	$20.00	$20.00	$20.00	$100.00
Price	$0.56	$7.29	$5.84	$0.54	$0.02	$85.02
Shares	35.71	2.74	3.42	37.04	1,000.00	1.18

* S&P 500 is treated as an imaginary no-load index fund priced at the index value.

You sell your shares on December 1, 2009, just in time to go holiday shopping. Your $100 investment has grown an astonishing $21,628.91, or 217.29 times your original investment! Forget that you didn't pay tax on the reinvested dividends or capital gains on the money—this is your fantasy and if these assumptions are good enough for finance professors selling books, it's good enough for you. Then you look back and wonder how much you could have gotten if you would have invested in the S&P 500 index (Table 1.2). If you would have bought the index and held it for the same time period, reinvesting all of the dividends, you only would have earned 1,211.57 percent. Not bad for 13.12 times your original $100 investment. But you only would have ended up with $1,311.57!

Table 1.2   Performance 1970–2010

	Stock portfolio	S&P 500*
Average monthly total return	1.13%	0.54%
Total return 1970-2010	21,628.91%	1,211.57%
Value in 1970	$100.00	$100.00
Value in 2010	$21,728.91	$1,311.57

* S&P 500 is treated as an imaginary no-load index fund priced at the index value.

But Wait There's More!

It's 1990 and your kids are older and grown up. They're all broke except for your son Cornelius, who wants to start investing like you did back in the day. Disneyland is certainly still around. Coca-Cola is still the preferred drink of the Magic Kingdom. Digital photography has not yet overtaken film. IBM miraculously has survived the death of mainframes and the birth of PCs. Since you smoked, there's a high likelihood that your children do as well.

Cornelius does the same thing that you did back in 1970. He invests $100 in these five stocks (and the results are going to be pretty good). Why only $100? It is 1990, and Cornelius is juggling debt, a mortgage, and still has to pay off his student loans to clown college. If it were 2010 he would be living at home begging you for the money. Only this time around, taxes can be avoided by investing in an IRA. By 1990, the wind is really at his back, because trades are cheaper from discount brokerage firms that didn't previously exist, he can defer taxes because IRAs existed after 1974, and it's easier to get the information to back-test investments, even before the Internet was widely used.

1990–2010 Results

In 1990, Cornelius calculates that with his $100 he can buy 2.76 shares of Disney, 1.23 shares of Eastman Kodak, 1.18 shares of IBM, 3.45 shares of Coca-Cola, and 19.23 shares of Philip Morris (Table 1.3). Just like you, his broker doesn't charge him any commissions. He doesn't have to pay any taxes when he reinvests the dividends because he's going to use an IRA. "Radical, this is closer to reality TV than Dad's stupid fantasy," he says to himself.

(Continued)

Table 1.3   Number of Shares Purchased on 1/2/1990 (Adjusted Closing Prices)

	Disney	Eastman Kodak	IBM	Coca-Cola	Philip Morris	S&P 500
Invest	$20.00	$20.00	$20.00	$20.00	$20.00	$100.00
Price	$7.24	$16.22	$17.01	$5.79	$1.04	$329.08
Shares	2.76	1.23	1.18	3.45	19.23	0.30

Cornelius is disciplined and he doesn't sell his shares until December 1, 2009, when he has to hit the malls to shop. Looking at his performance statement, he sees that his five stocks returned 680.85 percent (Table 1.4). His $100 has grown 7.81 times its value to $780.85. Like you, he decides to look and see how he would have done if he had invested in the S&P 500 over the same time period. Doing the math, he figures out that his $100 only would have grown to $338.85. That's a 238.85 percent return, or 3.39 times his original investment.

Table 1.4   Performance 1990–2010

	Stock portfolio	S&P 500
Average monthly total return	0.86%	0.51%
Total return 1990-2010	680.85%	238.85%
Value in 1990	$100.00	$100.00
Value in 2010	$780.85	$338.85

Is the Fantasy Waning?

It is hard to tell when experimenting with the same ridiculous hindsight setups that academics use to prove whatever point their research paper is trying to prove. What I am suggesting is simple. There is evidence—no matter where you look—that the big gains off the *super cycle* of the baby boomers of the United States are looking weaker going forward.

Time Is Not on Your Side

Over really long periods of time the capital markets—also known as the stock market—will grow. But, if you start at the wrong time, it could be a disaster. Even during a great century, there have been some bad times to buy a cross section of securities. Understand that

super cycle Technically an awesome bicycle you had as a child. It is also used as a slang term for a long economic cycle and is generally used to scare investors about any form of impending doom. Most recently, it's been used to describe the persistent increase in commodity prices. Super cycles are excellent sales tools due to their ultra-long time frame, allowing one to keep preaching a story regardless of the current environment.

Yes, you can chase China's growth or hot sectors like foreign search engines or social networking firms. The bottom line is too many people have too much information and all want the same thing—returns that are better than their peers. Put it this way. If more and more people get in the game, there is less for each person to take. The pie can only get cut up so many times. What is worse, the pie may not get bigger as more people take a slice. Nobody knows the future of investing, but as long as electronic trading lowers the barrier to entry, an endless stream of better players will look to take a piece of the action. At least the price of admission to the Magic Kingdom has only increased about 15 times since 1970, not the 60 times increase of the company's stock. The S&P 500's 12 times return would have left you a few bucks short of a ticket.

we are not talking about a single stock, but the market as a whole. Investing for the long term means you have to keep your money in the market and not take it out. Do you have the stamina to ride things out for 40 years? Remember to ask yourself, where are the Dutch, or where are the Romans? Do you think everything will just continue onward like it was over the last 100 years? If you have a long enough period of time you will make money, but if you think the next 40 years will be good you're betting that the next 40 years will continue to see the rise of the American economy. It's certainly not based on the rise of the Dutch Republic. There came a point even for the incredible Dutch East India Company that the luck ran out. By the time the New York Stock Exchange had a rented room to trade securities in back in 1792, the Dutch multinational was two years from being nationalized and on the way to liquidation. Do you want to start investing for the long term with a buy-and-hold approach during the last 50 years of the American Empire? There are a lot of parents and grandparents alive today who invested in the best 50 years of America, which was the last half of the twentieth century. If you're in the market for the next 10 years, good luck! You will need it. Most of the numbers that back up academic research on market returns show that only over a 30- to 40-year period will you be assured investing success no matter when you start. Consider how wonderful the last 50 years have been in America. Can it repeat? Most of my clients will need the next generation to bear witness to how things will turn out. If you want to beat the system, you need to have a healthy respect for the time you have and then invest accordingly. Let's go through three scary scenarios that will bring the idea back home. Then we can go forward with an attitude of self-preservation, not cheerleading.

Welcome Home, G.I.

It's 1950 and you have $10,000 to invest. Maybe you worked for it, and maybe you inherited the money, but you have it and want to set it aside for the long term. The war is over and confidence is returning to the global markets 20 years after the 1929 stock market crash. Your stock-broker sells you a *mutual fund,* or more likely a collection of stocks.

There was no way to invest in something that tracked an index at that time. You get the advice of buy and hold, which is fine since the 1929 crash is ancient history. Reinvest every dime and you will be healthy, wealthy, and wise.

By 1972 your $10,000 investment has grown to $175,160 after an impressive 18 percent increase that year! You read in the newspaper about how the S&P 500 only grew 3.56 percent in 1970, so this year you feel like you're in good financial shape. All those years of rein-vesting dividends since 1950 is starting to work out as retirement is looking closer to a reality. Come 1973, the S&P 500 is down 14.31 percent, and your investment has lost about $25,000 in value. It was a bad year for the stock market, but the worst of it has to be behind us, you say to yourself. Unfortunately for you, 1974 was an even worse year for the S&P 500, falling 25.9 percent. Your investment is now worth a little over $111,000, the same level it was at nine years ago! Either you're going to need to keep working, or your retirement life

mutual fund   A magic box that creates fees for Wall Street. Generally known as a professionally managed pool of money that invests in stocks and bonds. Mutual fund industry growth is one of the few charts that only go up. Currently, there are more mutual funds in America than there are stocks on the NYSE.

is going to be a little leaner than you had hoped it would be. What could work against you at this point is the fear of losing more money, dumping out right at the moment you need to stay in. Even if you stayed in the game and reinvested dividends, your portfolio would not start growing past the 1972 value until 1979. The high inflation rates of the late 1970s would rattle any investor, let alone someone who was getting ready to stop working and live off of their nest egg when prices are jumping up each year.

Bell Bottoms and VW Bugs

So you escape the 1973 to 1974 bear market with money to invest. Being young and enterprising you may have made money selling VW bugs during the Oil Embargo of 1973. Or, you could have recently sold a store that sold clothes to hippies and saw the writing on the wall before disco broke out. Both were good moves, but now there is money to invest and a future to save for. It is 1976 and you have $25,000. This time you can take advantage of buying the market as a whole, or maybe you still want to buy some stocks. What could go wrong now that the second worst bear market in the last 100 years is behind you? You've read about the S&P 500's 37 percent return last year, so you're ready to invest, and you're mentally prepared to buy and hope for a nice return in the long run. You're also planning to retire in 25 years, so you pat yourself on the back for being smart and thinking ahead.

By the end of the 1980s cars and music have culturally both gone down the tubes, but your $25,000 investment has grown to $179,912. The 1980s were a great decade for stocks, and you're hoping things will keep going like this through the 1990s. It turns out that the 1990s are even better than the 1980s, and at the end of 1999 your investment is worth more than $945,000! Rock has revived itself and Ferraris now start up in less than half the time. In short, it is a miracle. After a decade of hearing about how you would need to learn Japanese, now the mantra is all about the "Interweb" and the "www." You never thought you'd have this much money, and the more cautious side of you is starting to wonder how much longer this will last. But don't think too much about that, you tell yourself; you're in it for the long run. You're disappointed in 2000 when the S&P 500 drops 9.03 percent, but you remember how far you've come, so you try not to worry too much about it. You've always heard that it's bad to sell when the market goes down, so you decide to sit on your index fund, letting it grow. Since you are the buy and hold type, you never got involved in buying the tech-heavy Nasdaq Index. Avoiding fads has worked out so far. The S&P 500 drops another 11.85 percent in 2001, and then 21.97 percent in 2002. Your heart sinks when you find that your investment is now worth just $591,546. You were supposed to retire with that money! What are you going to do now? Hope that it goes up 75 percent next year? The next example will illustrate your wait time.

Knight Rider Crashes

After avoiding the horror of the 1970s stock market gyrations it seems like the worst may be over. While inflation is at a fever pitch, the market returned more than 18 percent in 1979. You inherit money from a rich uncle that made his fortune selling disco albums before an untimely death on the dance floor of Studio 54. It's 1980, the market is still cheap, and you have $40,000, so you buy an *index fund* that tracks the S&P 500.

Five years later you have more than doubled your money with $103,000 in your account. You think about spending the money. How about buying a 1985 Pontiac Trans Am so you can pretend you're David Hasselhoff driving around KITT, the famous talking car from the 1980s TV series *Knight Rider?* Okay, that may have been my personal fantasy in 1985, but you get the picture. You decide that it's better to have a comfortable retirement than Hollywood dreams. After all, you're in the stock market for the long haul.

By the end of the 1990s, your investment is worth more than one million dollars. After considering using the money to buy a new house, you get a mortgage and let the portfolio continue to grow.

---

index fund   A mutual fund that seeks to track the performance of a market index (e.g., S&P 500). Developed in 1973, index funds provide investors a way to trade broad indexes. Professional investors use index funds to capture the performance of a broad market without the cost of buying hundreds of stocks. Charlatans have been known to create mutual funds that try to beat the index, but are in fact simply "closet index funds." The most popular index funds are Exchange Traded Funds. See Chapter 8.

Between 2000 and 2002, the dot-com crash leaves you with just less than $651,000, and you're fuming. You had one million dollars just a few years ago! You tell yourself that you'll wait until the end of 2008 to retire, which should give you some time to get that money back. At the end of 2007, your investment is worth almost $1.2 million dollars, so you're not worried about retirement anymore. You remember back a few years ago after the dot.com crash, how you were down and out at just more than $651,000, and now you're sitting pretty. But wait a minute. Shouldn't you have more than $1.2 million? In 1999, you had just over one million dollars in the index fund. It's almost 10 years later and you've only gained about $200,000, or 13.72 percent. Looking at your statements, you earned 15.61 percent last year! Your head starts to hurt. Has the market gone nowhere since the beginning of the decade? Little did you know that next year, in 2008, the S&P 500 would plunge 36.58 percent. Out of frustration, you sell all of your shares at the end of the year for just more than $750,000. Looking at your statements from 1997 and 1998, you realize that you had about the same amount of money back then. Where did it all go? Aren't index funds supposed to be a good investment?

My Dinner with Burton

It was November of 2008 and I was invited to a due diligence conference in Boston. For those outside the Wall Street system, this is an event where a company flies you someplace nice and warm to hear them pitch a story under the cover of *education*. It was winter in Boston—you had to want to go to this one. My main reason for leaving the relatively decent weather in New Mexico was to hear Dr. Burton Malkiel speak. You may not know the name, but this guy is a legend in the business. An academic from Princeton, he wrote an amazing book called *A Random Walk Down Wall Street*. For years I hated this book with a passion. The bottom line, he says, is that you should simply buy and hold index mutual funds. How is this helpful to a guy like me who makes his money trying to beat the index? I was ready for a fight, or at least to have the opportunity to prove something to the guy who said my entire life's work was for nothing.

I arrived late, notably because I was talking with Dr. Andrew Lo, the guy who taught me risk budgeting and the basis of the work we do at my firm. Walking through the banquet door were no more than 150 top movers and shakers in the adviser world—a small group for the level of the speaker. I knew I was here because somebody thought I had a chance in this industry, or they just wanted to sell me their products. More likely it was the latter. There was only one table with a few empty seats. I sat down and introduced myself to the other guests. To my utter terror I realized I was sitting next to Burton himself! No, I didn't know what he looked like. Quickly after the introductions, the host started talking and I just sat there quietly. Once Burton took the podium there was a flurry of notes written on the back of every cocktail napkin I could get a hold of. He was wrong! His whole talk referenced the timing of the current global crisis, opportunities to make money on the panic, and his views of China. I knew I had this guy and I was going to expose him for not following his own rules. After working myself into a fever, the talk ended, the applause subsided, and the perfunctory line of glad handers and questioning began. I waited until most of the people had cleared out before I came into the kill zone.

Burton knew before I started talking what I wanted. I said clearly, you seem to think that is possible to beat the index—tell me I am wrong. He was cool, calm, and collected. He said if you are above average and have a little luck you can outperform any benchmark, and he wasn't even trying to get rid of me! We talked for a while about my style, and he encouraged me to keep trading and create a long-term track record. His message was simple—most people, statistically, can't beat the markets. Everyone can't win, right? Since most investors don't have the time or skill to dedicate their lives to this ridiculous game, how else can I outperform unless they underperform? He had me and knew it. His tips were simple: find markets that are less picked over, more illiquid, and most importantly, inefficient.

Before he moved on, I asked how he made his money. Simple, he said: book royalties, warehouse properties (getting 8 percent and more at the time), and small cap Chinese stocks. This was it! I thanked him and told him I was going to go home to my wife and tell her it was okay that I didn't buy and hold, and Dr. Burton Malkiel approved this message.

I left the banquet room knowing one thing: Forget what they say, watch what they do. Burton wasn't an index investor; his money was in peddling ideas. He admitted that there could be some inefficiency and to this day he remains the chief investment officer of AlphaShares Investments, pushing China as the growth story of the world.

Now that the boogieman was confronted I could move on to greener pastures. There was no random walk, rational world, or anything else that could convince me that buy and hold would ever work. I was free. I started to look at the other guys that have espoused the buy and hope, the "you can never beat the market so join it" clan. Dr. Eugene Fama was the next person to track down. After reading through his works, many which are required reading for the Chartered Financial Analyst (CFA) examinations, I came across a simple truth: Fama is in the business of selling mutual funds. His firm, Dimensional Fund Advisers, or DFA, ran more than $200 billion in index funds as of 2010. These guys practically invented the market. Every stone I turned revealed the same story. Even in academia the game is rigged—they want your money.

Lie of the Pie

In the last chapter I was freed from the tyranny of a buy-and-hope philosophy. To attract more individual investors, Wall Street started to come up with more sophisticated ways to sell strategies. It was not enough to find the hot new list of stocks, but a method of delivering a cohesive idea to the individual investor without having to interest them in individual stocks. Most people just want a way to save for retirement. The fear of making a wrong move or losing money playing a game of picking stocks was a turnoff that needed a solution. This chapter is all about the way Wall Street took some academic ideas and twisted them to sell people securities. Not only that, the very concept of diversification and asset allocation was turned into a sales pitch that after 1987 started to develop cracks in its foundation. A new take on risk—or perhaps the proper one in the first place—is outlined so you can control it.

Today's Outrage: Pie Town

It makes me sick to see pie charts and asset allocation pimped out to the average investor. What makes it worse is when I ask the average investor why they have a particular allocation, and they clearly don't know how it was selected for them. Sure, they will say they told the broker they want to be conservative, or grow the money, or my personal favorite, "make as much as you can without loss." It is as clear as day that nobody cares to do their homework and face the facts. Often it is too complicated for investors to know where to start. Not to mention money is the most sensitive part of people's

adviser   Traditionally a person of trust, this term was altered to include any stockbroker that wanted to improve his or her image after the dot-com crash. While generally unclear to the public, an adviser is anybody that makes money from people while handling their investments. This includes those of the highest fiduciary standards, like a Registered Investment Adviser (RIA). It also can refer to a broker that sells high-priced variable annuities with an 8 percent commission, but has a business card that says "trusted adviser."

lives. Wall Street is obsessed with telling the institutional crowd how to manage their risk, then lies to the retail crowd about how to construct a portfolio. When you are an institutional investor, most of the time there are far more sophisticated tools available that will help the big players know almost daily how much money they have at risk and what could go wrong. None of it is based on some pie chart. Understand that none of these powerful tools guarantee success, but they at least give the big players some insight into what they are getting themselves into. Many so-called *advisers* buy into the myth of the pie chart simply because it is easy.

Even if they have access to sophisticated tools, educating clients and learning how to apply it to individual portfolios is too much for some advisers. If your job is to sell products, innovation can scare off the very people that need it most. I want to point out to the public how there are very specific problems with the methods used to explain risk to investors.

The first clue that you need to upgrade your adviser is simple: A pie chart is used. Rarely will you see a pie chart being used by someone who studies statistics. One of the reasons is that people don't perceive a visual area as well as they perceive length. There are some theories about this, including Stevens' power law. It suggests that people don't see visual space like in a pie chart as accurately as they do length. A simple bar chart is easier for a human to decipher as shown in Figure 2.1. I think pie charts are the preferred method of delivering information because they are visually pleasing and suggest a cohesive unit to talk about. Even I use them out of convention. So, we need to know how a widely used tool can mislead our senses.

The individual investor is told asset allocation is diversifying a portfolio among different types of *asset classes* such as stocks, bonds,

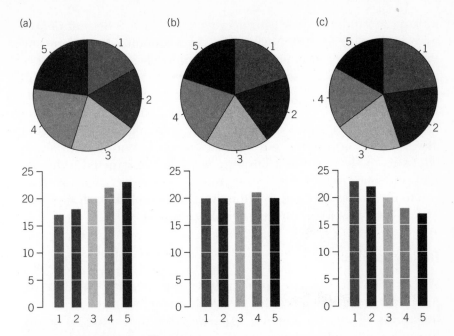

Figure 2.1   Pie Charts vs. Bar Charts
Source: http://upload.wikimedia.org/wikipedia/commons/thumb/b/b4/Piecharts
.svg/2000px-Piecharts.svg.png

---

asset class   Describes the general type of asset in the context of a portfolio. Stocks, bonds, real estate, and commodities are the most common portfolio assets for investors. However, asset classes also include stamp collections, Beanie Babies, and private equity. Usually used by advisers to impress clients with the broad diversification of terms a single asset class can be split up into. This aids in selling more mutual funds with different asset classes. For example, U.S. stocks can be split up into large-cap growth, large-cap value, large-cap high-dividend yield, and large-cap sector-that-is-currently-going-up which you don't own because your sector is going down.

---

and cash. Advisers always try to make a big deal out of some assets such as international stocks and commodities because they have become much more in vogue this past decade.

The pitch continues that the classes do not move in tandem, but in a random walk unrelated to each other. A random walk is an overused term. Does anyone really think global markets are just walking around aimlessly with no rhyme or reason? Several people have been awarded the Nobel Prize in Economics for suggesting this. Perhaps the winners are chosen randomly as well. Of course, all of these asset classes are expected to go up over time. You wouldn't buy something if it wasn't designed to make a profit, right? Because they don't move together, one asset will surely be moving up while another moves down. Thus, we have a group of different assets that all go up in the long run, but their random movement allows us to sleep at night knowing we have constructed a diversified portfolio. All you need is a professional adviser that can lead you to the Promised Land by telling you how much of each asset you should have based on the level of risk appropriate.

The Original Pie Crust

Where did this idea of diversification come from? In 1952 an American economist named Harry Markowitz wrote an article describing "Portfolio Theory." To save you the hassle of going through the formulas, let me explain it this way: If you hold combinations of securities that don't correlate, you can decrease your risk to the risk of a single asset. It is another way of saying not to put all your eggs in one basket. Only in this instance, you have other things besides eggs. At the time this was a huge idea, but it has a few problems when it's used in the real world. Modern Portfolio Theory (MPT) assumes that investors will be rational. If given two portfolios with the same expected return, an investor will choose the less risky one. Why would you choose something more risky if it does the same thing as another portfolio with less risk? You wouldn't if there was a bulletproof way of knowing the risk return of every security. People have different opinions on the matter. What makes the whole exercise of finding the less risky portfolio more dubious is that we use past performance to get this so-called expected return. Did I mention that there is no one way of coming up with this number? There is a whole army of analysts—including people like me—that have our own special ways of guessing what an asset class is expected to do in the future. If any one of us really knew how to do it, we would be on a private island with a Lamborghini to drive around on the beach.

You can read a ton of books on the subject, but many are critical of MPT because it doesn't reflect the reality of how the market actually behaves. Why? Because people don't always act rationally and never have. Plus, if we all put our portfolios together perfectly, it would distort the effect. The added value of MPT won't work if everybody does it. Put another way, if you knew the shortest line at the amusement park, what would happen if all of the other people knew this information too? Anything that really works well will start to erode as others hop on the train. This descent of rational behavior started to rear its head after the 1987 stock market crash. MPT is based on something called Gaussian distribution. Yes, there was a German by the name of Carl Friedrich Gauss who came up with a method of statistics back in 1809. He was not a stock market trader to my knowledge. I blame Gauss in general for the unrealistic bell curves that are taught in finance departments in universities. If you use Gaussian distribution, it will give you an idea of how much the market will move one way or another over a given period of time. However, we learned on October 19, 1987 that the drop in the markets was equal to a 20-standard-deviation move that was only supposed to occur once every 4.5 billion years. In other words, if you used simple bell curves three standard deviations would cover 99.7 percent of the movement in the market. A 22 percent drop in one day was so far out on the bell curve it was simply off the charts.[1]

Because the 1987 crash was near impossible if you assumed that people were rational and obeyed bell curves, it was open season on the whole theory. My beef with MPT is not the theory, but how it is used to sell people ideas that don't work. At the core, we simply need to remember MPT is all about lowering risk using things that move differently—now that is brilliant!

Wall Street asks investors a different question: What is the appropriate level of risk you are willing to take? That must mean that risk is a major determining factor in return. But no, according to the asset allocator, your return is always based on the asset class. This is simply madness, and as you will see later, the pie charts adjusted for risk look very different. This affects investors that don't have a full understanding of where their return comes from. Meaning, you make or lose money based on the risk you take, which you express by making bets on certain asset classes. So, why does Wall Street try to gloss over the risk part and just focus on the asset class?

It all came about with a 1986 study by Brinson, Hood, and Beebower (BHB). Everyone talks about the study but most never read it or understand what is in it. These guys looked at 91 pension funds from 1974 to 1983. It was not a very long study, but they got the idea that if you just replaced the holdings with that of an asset class (think index fund versus *active management*) you would have been better off. People have been arguing about this study for years, since it implies active management is a waste of time and money. It was a thorn in the side of pension fund managers that were simply buying the market, charging a fee, and underperforming.

To add fuel to the fire, another follow-up study was done in 2000, this time by Ibbotson and Kaplan, which came up with similar results. The battle here is not worth fighting. It is essentially two groups. One wants to convince you that an index or *passive approach* is best. The other wants to convince you that the market can be beaten.

Most of the time it is suggested that the market can be beaten by selecting better companies within a certain index universe. Oh boy—my stocks are better than your stocks—are we on the playground? I say don't bother. Neither method deals with the key issue of risk, nor how it changes over time. Both camps use the same assumptions.

active investing   Referred to as the American way of life, or pursuit of beating the market. By making active buy-and-sell decisions, the active investor attempts to generate higher returns than the market index. While most active investors fail in beating the market, it is human nature to try and defeat most other people. Notable winners include Warren Buffet and Peter Lynch. Losers include most active mutual fund managers.

passive investing   An investing strategy that buys and holds low-cost index funds to closely match the market returns. By admitting you don't want to go for the gold, a passive investor wins by choosing to be mediocre. Most American passive investors fail, though, by not being able to stick with the strategy during exceptionally good or bad periods in market performance due to the inherent manifest destiny gene. Notable winners include active investors that write books on the virtues of passive investing.

What are the assumptions?

1. That asset classes will not move in tandem with each other.
2. That each class has a unique thing called *expected return*, and somehow smart people know what this number is and it is expected to happen.
3. That expected return is the holy grail of portfolio construction.

The passive camp then goes on to show that most investors can't beat the market. It's an easy stat to come up with since everyone can't beat the market at the same time just as we all can't be at the top of the class. The only way around this is for everyone to do the exact same thing. Then we could all be average together. This is what the passive camp is really suggesting. Active investment fans will show a list of superior investment results from star managers, or simply say "Warren Buffet" and rest their case. But remember, they are simply suggesting that you should diversify your investments using the same pie charts, but with managers that actively choose the stocks versus a simple index of all of the stocks. Why? The thinking is that if you can pick the best and leave out the duds, you will beat the market. Yeah, sign me up for that! I used to fight the fight and try to make my case, but in the end realized that it was not an argument that would ever be won.

Breaking Eggs, Then the Entire Kitchen

I deal in the real world and don't have the luxury of investing in a rational market found only in the halls of finance departments at universities. For years I tried to practice MPT. It even comes with a few reasonable strategies that make it exciting to clients. You could try the static approach by simply establishing the right mix, and *rebalance* the portfolio each year. Why? So you can keep the pie chart constant.

Next, you can go for the tactical approach. You tell your client small cap is going to be great this year and overweight it, then next year say small cap is bad, very bad, and we should have less. Big firms love this because it makes the client feel that people are doing things behind the scenes, but not so much that their pie chart doesn't always have a little bit of everything. That way when

> **rebalancing**   In order to justify paying a fee to an adviser, rebalancing must occur. When the market, for whatever reason, changes or moves in price the adviser must then rebalance the portfolio to some predetermined ratio. Sophisticated managers actually decide how to allocate capital, not rebalance to a fixed model. However, the term is still used to describe the active movement of asset classes within a portfolio. Similar to the adviser definition, the quality of rebalancing is a mile wide and an inch deep, technically speaking.

you are wrong, it is only a little bit off from your "long term goal of financial freedom." This one worked well for me, but I was actually trying to beat the market. While I was okay at it I never had consistent outperformance that I felt was repeatable. Plus, my outperformance was based on either picking a dog or catching a hot market. This was too little science and too much gut instinct. How could I be confident in my actions long term? In the end it was just playing around with a static strategy. Pathetic. You may hear this being sold as a *core and explore* strategy. Advisers will tell you to keep about 70 percent in core assets and explore with 30 percent. This is just a clever way of saying you are using a tactical strategy, but usually it comes with some expensive mutual funds to manage the *exploration*. Been there, done that.

The last strategy to mention is more diverse. It may involve buying and selling assets based on the trend of the market. Add to assets that are on the move and sell those that are in the pits. You can be a contrarian and do the opposite. Some people may call this trend or countertrend, but it is simply a more dynamic way of buying the same pie chart. This last approach is how I trade. While you do better finding the big trend, money can be made a dozen different ways as long as you have a plan. However, as long as you are managing money without the risk component, you never get to the heart of the matter.

You see, Wall Street wants to fill your mind with all of the neat asset classes they have to sell. Need a shot in the arm? Why not add some small-cap emerging markets? Feeling scarred? Why not sell that broad-based mutual fund and get with blue chip dividend payers? Let's not even get into the world of commodities or complex strategies. If the industry can convince you only to think of the asset class's expected return, you are then tuned into their prognostications of what those returns will be. The pie chart is just the delivery system, like a cigarette. Now, with your handy little allocation and risk tolerance given to you by a trusted adviser, you are free to roam the garbage dumps of Wall Street noise to find your golden goose. Will it be Eastern Europe that boosts your returns this year, or perhaps a bet on China? What would otherwise look like reckless abandon is now fully sanctioned by Wall Street. You have a pie chart, so why worry?

I will tell you why to worry: Risk, correlation, and the false sense of security that you can drop anything into your pie chart as long as the asset class matches the slot. In order to move forward I need to go back. Everything I needed to learn about risk and portfolio construction I learned on the mean streets of Manhattan years ago as a young trader on Wall Street. Remember that in the 1990s the Internet existed, as did E-Trade, but people were not doing everything online like they do now. You really want to trust your trade to a 56k dial up connection on AOL? Back then people called a broker and placed orders. I started my career writing paper tickets in triplicate and running them to a cage. No, I didn't have my own runner and never did; I ran faster and could bum rush the other guys if needed.

At the time tech stocks were all the rage, and everyone wanted the big returns they promised. The problem was that some moved a lot faster than my clients could handle. Sure, clients wanted to make a lot of money, but when they called in for a quote or checked the ticker on CNBC, they didn't want to see really big movements. So, I looked for the tech companies that were hot, but didn't move as much per day as others. If I had only known what I was onto back then! Usually the bigger names that had earnings made better candidates as long as they were involved with anything dot-com related. In essence, I was looking for stocks that had a high expected return, but didn't have high volatility. This worked for a while, but one day I asked a senior broker (who later blew up his entire book of business with a penny stock during the tech wreck) for advice on how to do well in the business. Keep in mind everyone around me was doing well, it was the roaring 90s, but I knew it would not last forever. He said, "Simple—show growth every year." That was it! Make the accounts go up and don't lose money. You win some, you lose some. Just hit singles all day and forget the home runs. This was a relief since everyone around me was looking for the next 10-to-1 Internet company.

From there on I worked on what are now considered simple hedging strategies but were pretty advanced for my average client. In a nutshell, I would buy a hot stock and then write an option that would provide some downside protection while limiting my upside. After a while clients were comfortable with the strategy and referred their friends and family to me. Looking back, I am not sure if they really understood what I was doing, or if they simply liked the confidence and passion in my voice. Either way, my commissions went up (more trades meant more money), and clients had some protection when the market made those nasty little bumps along the way. The problem was stocks that had the biggest bang for your buck on these option contracts were also the most volatile. This was a classic mistake. You get a new toy that works well, has lots of promise, and always works as long as the market goes up. Sounds like the housing bubble years later.

So, in the search to control and lower my risk, I ended up increasing it in the end. Why? Because I was hitting singles all day—with grenades! I was trading the high-flying stocks of the time. While it was better than just buying and dying, a prudent hedging strategy doesn't work when you start off with crazy stocks. Then there was the small problem of correlation. That is the fancy word that tells us how much one thing moves with another. Today Wall Street loves to pitch institutional investors *non-correlated* assets, and boy can we use them. In a globalized investing world it gets harder and harder to find stuff that doesn't move the same way all the time. Want to get my attention? Just say "it doesn't correlate" and I stop to turn around. For the retail crowd, they just flat out lie and say asset classes don't move together when most totally mimic each other. I don't know how they continue to get away with this. Perhaps they think you will never look anything up or ask a pro that has skin in the game. Or maybe they think if they tell you asset allocation is a theory of mixing non-correlating assets (things that don't move in tandem) you will assume the things they sell you are actually non-correlating. Thirty years ago small-cap and large-cap stocks didn't move together all the time. It took years for everyone to buy into the pie chart, but after a while everyone owns a bit of everything and the effect wears off. As you are starting to catch on—most things correlate with each other.

Getting back to my problem back in tech land, when I looked at the portfolios, everything lacked diversification. Just because you owned a software firm, a chipmaker, and a money-losing dot-com

retailer didn't mean you were diversified. Why? It didn't have anything to do with the fact that these were all Internet or tech-oriented
companies. It was that they moved together. This is where Wall
Street confuses investors and gets them off their dime. They tell you
to diversify, either by way of asset class or sector. For instance, you
might be told to buy small-cap stocks to diversify your large-cap holdings, or maybe to have some health care stocks to balance out your
energy companies. Tell me this is useful when the S&P 500 is down
5 percent on the day. Sure, there will be some things that will do
well, but nothing you can consistently take to the bank. At the very
minimum, we all need to look at our portfolios and make sure they
are diversified in terms of their correlation. This is not as simple as
it may seem. A beer company's stock may move in the same direction as a firm that makes beer cans. If you can simply look at the
statistical relationship, or the correlation over a period of months or
a few years, it is easy to see if the market, not Wall Street, is moving
the stocks in tandem or not.

Investors also need to change the way they look at their portfolios from a high level, not simply as compilations of securities. This
starts by looking at the risk and not at the asset classes. If I told you
international stocks correlated with the domestic markets 90 percent of the time, would you still be hot to add them? Maybe, but
you probably wouldn't see them as a diversification silver bullet. If
I told you the 20 percent allocation to emerging markets contributed 50 percent of the risk in your portfolio, would you draw your
pie chart differently? Wall Street hopes you don't ask or answer
those types of questions, but I will—right here, right now!

We are starting to get a clear picture of what is wrong with the
system. Risk is important, but we are told a diverse mix will cure
it. Plus, did you pick up that the pie chart doesn't say that the risk
of the assets can change over time? Or, are they just using a long-
term average of risk and leaving out those confusing little details
like year-to-year reality? Wasn't Bank of America a little crazier in
2008 than McDonalds?

The chart shown in Figure 2.2 shows you only one thing—
different stock markets move in tandem today. Domestic (S&P
500), international (EFA), emerging markets (EEM), and small cap
(Russell 2000) are supposed to give investors diversification according to MPT. Looking at the five-year correlation suggests that they
may be doing less than you think, versus a Treasury that has a clear

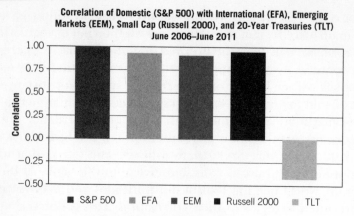

Figure 2.2   One of These Things Is Not Like the Other

diversifying effect on a portfolio. Over time these markets have started to move together from what I can only guess is from the globalization of our planet. I wish that wasn't true. Back when I was a stockbroker the first thing I was told to ask a prospective client was if they bought big board or OTC. The big board was a reference to the NYSE, or large blue chip stocks that normally would pay a dividend and were perceived as less risky. The OTC or Over the Counter part simply referred to small-cap stocks. The NASDAQ was still a new idea back then and the only real company on it was Microsoft. (My Dad used to tell me he liked that company, but never wanted to buy it because it was not listed on a real exchange.) These were usually new, risky, and exciting firms that didn't pay dividends for the most part and had a completely different following than the blue chip lovers. Back then you had two different types of investors. They looked at markets differently, didn't move the same way, and caused the non-correlating effect that the pie chart is supposed to have. If only we could go back in time and separate investors into their respective clans, then the pie chart might look a little less stupid.

So, What Is Next? Risk Budgeting!

There was always something eating away at me when working though different trading strategies versus investment theories. All traders are concerned about is risk. Like gambling, traders look at what you have to put up and what you can get, or simple odds. Investment theories were always trying to compete for the expected return of the bet. This is when I started to listen more carefully to what Dr. Andrew Lo, a thought leader on hedge funds and financial engineering from the MIT Sloan School of Finance, was trying to get across. A peddler of ideas himself, he came up with Adaptive Market Hypothesis. I don't know why it is a hypothesis—it's simple. Survival is the game, and the game changes with each new crop of investors. Academia is not wrong, it is just too slow to adapt to the reality on the ground. And anything that is working well will stop working at some point in time. Risk it seems is the only thing we should be looking at, not some old idea about what the stock market returned in the past. To add to my interest after my influential after-dinner conversation with Dr. Burton Malkiel, Lo wrote the controversial *A Non-Random Walk Down Wall Street* in 1999. This was my type of academic.

Why do you care? When you build a portfolio, you have a limited budget for risk. Anyone can say they want as much return as they can get, but when asked about how much they could stand to lose, nobody says as much as they have or more. Sure, you have degenerate gamblers that will risk it all, but the average person reading this book is probably not willing to risk it all. Wall Street specializes in getting you to agree to expected returns with the secondary factor of how much risk you have to take. This is why they invented pie charts. You pick the one that satisfies how much money you want to make relative to the other pies.

Figure 2.3 shows a typical lineup of pie charts that advisers or brokers will show clients along with some long-term historical returns. By the end of this chapter I will show you what is really going on, but for now just stay warm and fuzzy. Table 2.1 shows a summary of the average annual returns for each pie chart.

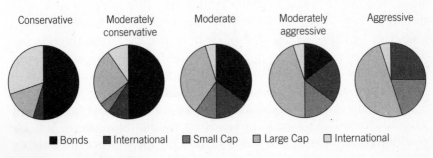

Figure 2.3   Typical Pie Charts

Table 2.1   Average Annual Returns

	Conservative	Moderately conservative	Moderate	Moderately aggressive	Aggressive
Average annual return (1970– 2006)	8.60%	9.80%	10.60%	11.10%	11.40%

Each investor tells their adviser things like, "I am young, so let's pick the pie chart with the most risk since I don't need the money." Or, "I am old, so let's pick the more conservative pie chart." Most people, in my experience, will choose the middle pie, moving up or down a notch depending if the market recently performed well (they will choose the moderately aggressive) or poorly (they will choose the moderately conservative). The critical error is that nobody is dealing with risk head on. Let's change that.

If we have a limit on how much actual risk we want to take, then it is finite. Expected return, while based on risk, should simply be thought of as some type of expectation or guess for what we may or may not get for the finite amount of risk we take. Thus, expected return is a secondary factor, not the main component we are being sold by Wall Street. If risk is now the main ingredient, why shouldn't we build portfolios around it? Let me give you a simple example.

We all know that each day we take in a finite amount of calories, sometimes more than we should. When it comes to money, though, we need to have some type of disciplined routine or we will end up emaciated or exploding from risk. So, you go to the doctor and are told to take in 1,000 calories a day by eating a delicious one-pound steak. I don't mean to offend vegetarians, this is not a real steak nor does a great rib eye have only 1,000 calories. The doctor even gives you a picture of the type of steak so you can go to the butcher and get it with ease. One day you see the butcher and ask for your daily dose of beef. He tells you that while this one-pound steak is just like the one in the picture, the cow ate something strange and it is clocking in at 2,000 calories. You ask him why, but he can only prognosticate like the talking heads on CNBC! Stop there. You are disciplined and this is not a real steak. Quickly you ask the butcher to cut the steak in half, you only need 1,000 calories. He rolls his eyes and gives you half. That's your loss, right? The next day (or market condition), you come in and ask for your usual 1,000-calorie one-pound steak. The butcher apologizes and says the cow must have eaten some form of diet feed, because the one-pound steak clocked in at only 500 calories. You tell him you are not a movie star preparing for a role. You want 1,000 calories. The butcher gets the message and wraps up not one, but two steaks and sends you on your way.

This is the core of rational discipline in investing! Ask any professional trader and this will not come as any surprise; a trader manages risk, regardless of the package it comes in. Now let's use another example. If your portfolio is supposed to be 100 percent in the stock market and suddenly, because of global events, like an earthquake or because somebody on CNBC (including me!) said something, and the market becomes twice as risky as it has been in the past, you should only hold half as much in stock. It doesn't matter why it is more risky, let me handle that when I talk to reporters, I can make it sound exciting. What you are doing is keeping your risk the same, not timing the market or trying to beat anything. Let the market do the work, if it wants to be hopped up on goofballs, ease up on the gas. If the market is significantly less volatile than it has been historically, then you can afford to take on more exposure, by owning more high-risk assets like emerging markets or small-cap index funds.

How you accomplish this is your choice, but the basic philosophical tenet of survival is universal. Wall Street doesn't want you thinking of risk, or you would laugh in its face when told to "hang in there" when risk shot up. Stick with a long-term risk budget, not a long-term static pie chart that could end up jacking up your portfolio with more risk than a Vegas gambler. On the other side, clear skies are a time to enjoy the sunshine. Sticking to a strategy that limits profits when markets are less risky just holds you back, no matter if you are conservative or aggressive. It is about risk, nontandem things, and their expected return. We don't need to throw out MPT because risk and correlations change. All we do is keep it updated. We are living in a fast world. Wall Street hates this because it makes us less interested in what they are selling at the time and more interested in what we need at the moment.

What We Trade Is Fear Itself

Figure 2.4 is a chart of volatility and the stock market. The main takeaway is that when things get volatile, you should start paying attention.

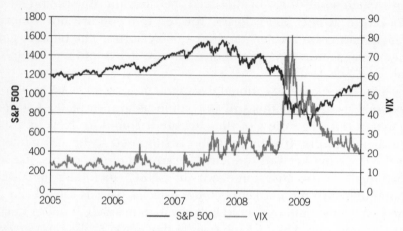

Figure 2.4   Volatility Versus S&P 500 2005–2009

Volatility is commonly measured by the Market Volatility Index (VIX). The important thing to know about the VIX is that it is concerned wholly with the future. It is a measure of how the market is expected to act based on how many people are buying options and futures. Sound complex? Well, try this out. You own a house next to a river. This year, the weather is sunny and dry, and you know what? Last year it was the same, and the year before that. In fact, it has been sunny and dry so long that even Gramps can't remember a rainy season. Are you going to buy flood insurance? NO! Let's face it—you'd be wasting your money. So now it starts to rain, just a little bit. You shrug it off. Suddenly it turns into an unrelenting deluge. You call up your insurance company but the insurance company can see it raining too, and the flood insurance rates have tripled overnight. Suddenly you are faced with a tough decision: Do you wait out the rain and hope it stops, or do you buy the inflated insurance price? So what do you do? Being a savvy homeowner, you talk the insurance agent into a deal. It goes like this: I will buy your insurance at the current price if it continues to rain for another x-amount of days (the strike price), however, I reserve the right to walk away from this deal at anytime. The insurance agent is no dummy, and he accepts the deal with the caveat that you have to pay him a non-refundable fee upfront (a premium). Now you are happy because you have the ability to buy insurance if the rain continues, but you don't have to buy it if the rain stops. The insurance man is happy because he isn't expecting it to keep raining and he just took your money. You just executed a "put-option."

The VIX measures how many people are buying insurance—options—and uses that information to produce an index of market volatility. Once again: If investors are confident in the market, the price of options goes down—the weather is sunny and no one wants insurance. If investors are afraid that the market will fall, the price of options goes up (the rain starts to fall) as people scramble to hedge against a bear market. It is for this reason that the VIX has earned the reputation as the Fear Index.

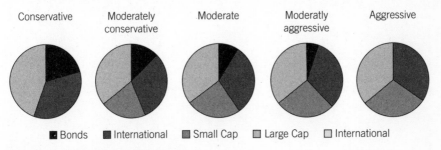

■ Bonds   ■ International   ■ Small Cap   ☐ Large Cap   ☐ International

Figure 2.5   Risk-Adjusted Pie Charts
Just for the curious, the last set of pie charts in Figure 2.5 uses the square of the standard deviation (variance), multiplied by the proportion of asset class in the portfolio. The product of each asset is then square-rooted to give the standard deviation (risk) with respect to the portfolio.

Now, let's take a look at a few more pie charts shown in Figure 2.5, but this time measuring the amount of risk each asset class is contributing to the mix.

As you can see if this was what your adviser explained when you first walked in, you may have had a few more questions about what it was going to take to get the return you wanted, or how much work it would take to keep the portfolio stable. In the case of the conservative portfolio, most of the risk is coming from large and international stocks. While the aggressive portfolio has risk fairly evenly spread between large, small, and international stocks, though the actual percentage per class is different. Essentially, a small amount of small cap stocks makes a big contribution to risk.

Now do you see why it is important to look at risk, rather than just slots in the pie chart that can be interchanged with whatever new mutual fund is on the hot list? Diversification does work, but not if we forget to keep the risk constant. There is no point to having different things in your portfolio if not to reduce risk. Asset allocation in only the first step in figuring out how much of different types of securities make a portfolio that suits your risk budget. The alchemy must be constantly reviewed, not set in stone via a pie chart. Just remember, you have a limited amount of calories, so keep counting.

PART

II

WALL STREET: THE SET UP

3

Mayday

Regulatory changes were made in the 1970s in the interest of increasing market fairness. One of the unintended consequences of making markets more accessible was lower profit margins for brokerage firms. Brokerage firms had to adapt to new models in order to keep sucking money out of investors' pockets. It takes a village. The Securities and Exchange Commission (SEC) had to be brought in to help with the injustice of price compression. Let's look back at the laws that created this injustice of declining profits and how the industry fought back.

How the SEC Let the Dogs In

Sometimes the best intentions of regulators backfire. Even when it is clear to the industry what is being said, the general public rarely has the background to make informed decisions. Add to that the desire to make a sale and not educate the consumer on regulation. Before we get into this mess, understand that most of the rules put forth by the SEC are there to protect the consumer. I am not saying that to avoid making them mad at me, but after the SEC's complete failure to detect the Madoff scandal in 2008, it's important to understand what it is and what it does. The SEC is there to make sure everyone plays fair, but keep in mind nobody can protect you from being a bad consumer. This is at the core of how some specific rules were passed by the SEC to make Wall Street a better place. Problem is, Wall Street is in a perpetual game of cat and mouse, with the regulators always behind.

What Is the SEC?

After the crash of 1929 and the Great Depression of the early 1930s, Congress put into law the Securities Act of 1933. In a nutshell this forced companies to register with the Securities and Exchange Commission, or SEC, in order to sell securities. Prior to that the responsibility fell on each state, which even today would be a mess, let alone with the primitive communication back then. Just look at the hassle of getting a driver's license. This is an example of a right still issued by states. And for the record, insurance salespeople still have to register with each state. I believe the insurance industry is such a mess that I would have to write another book just to scratch the surface.

Now that we had new laws on the books, we had to actually create the SEC. The Securities Exchange Act of 1934 created the federal agency that is primarily responsible for enforcing and regulating the securities industry. In 1940, the SEC would be tasked with regulating mutual funds and investment advisers. The Sarbanes-Oxley Act of 2002 and the Credit Rating Agency Reform Act in 2006 also added to its duties. Yet, the last act didn't stop the abuse it was supposed to curb when the subprime mortgage markets blew up, only to find that the issuers of the mortgage-backed securities had AAA *credit ratings* from the top ratings agencies.

> **credit rating**   Somewhere between an estimation to an outright lie of the credit worthiness of a corporation or country. Different than the highly irritating and often inaccurate personal credit scores, this type of rating is done by actual people, not computers. A good rating suggests less risk of default. A low score suggests a high risk of default. They are not investigative reporters. They take regular, known information and analyze it relative to other securities. When an agency issues a credit rating downgrade it signals that everyone on the planet is finally in agreement something is wrong.

While there are numerous failures on the SEC's part, we do need some form of government enforcement. Just remember that like any government agency, they are held back by red tape and funding. If there is a known issue and you need to complain about a fraud, they are the people you contact. After helping several attorneys understand securities law cases, my anecdotal evidence is simple. The SEC is capable of taking down the bad guys if it wants to, but there are simply not enough agents to police the whole industry. In order to police stockbrokers, the SEC relies on the Financial Industry Regulatory Authority (FINRA) to enforce the rules. Some people don't like this because FINRA is a private corporation that self-regulates the industry. Being involved in the industry as long as I have, it is generally agreed that when push comes to shove and you sue a bad broker, FINRA generally comes down on the side of the customer. Rigged? Not from what I can see, as the real problems stem from the practices that land brokers in FINRA arbitration hearings.

Mayday, We Have Soft Dollars!

May Day 1975 was not just another celebration of international workers or ancient pagan rituals. It was the day the SEC ended fixed commission rates on national exchanges. Rule 19b-3 sent destructive capitalism to the old school Wall Street. Prior to May Day, *broker-dealers* didn't compete on price, but on what they offered a client that nobody else did.

Back then most of the folks buying and selling stock were not individual investors, but institutional managers that ran pensions and mutual funds. Since the price to trade a stock was the same no matter where you went, institutional research was the main factor that determined who received the commission. Everyone freaked out. If we entered a new era that would ultimately lead to a race to the cheapest trade, how could proprietary research continue? On top of that, what about institutional money managers who found certain brokers insightful, but had a fiduciary responsibility to seek the best *execution* and lowest trading rates?

There was so much screaming that Congress made an amendment that would address these issues. Section 28(e) is known as the safe harbor provision that allows money managers to pay more for trades. In order to understand why this was important at the time, but problematic today, we need to understand how things worked back then.

broker-dealer   A company that trades securities, either for customers or for its own account. When executing a trade for a client, the firm is acting as a broker. When trading for its own account, the firm is acting as a dealer. There have been some instances of broker-dealers dealing against customers by front running their orders or otherwise using their information to trade against them. There is a fine line between illegal front running and simply mining data from customers for a dealer's proprietary trading operations.

execution   Term to describe the obligation of your broker-dealer to provide the best price on your transaction. This is a subjective term using several inputs, including the speed of filling your order, getting a better price than was quoted, and the ability to justify higher commissions to clients for using a particular broker. Electronic trading has made best execution an arms race of complex routers and algorithms.

In theory, money managers should use a brokerage firm to execute trades and independent research groups to gain market insight. It never worked that way. Back in 1975, there were only a handful of independent research firms like Standard and Poor's or Value Line. This was great for a beginning investor looking for an easy way to look at a stock chart or measure earnings. The big boys wanted more, and generic stock reports didn't cut it. Plus, the top talent at the time was attracted to the high pay of brokerage firms' research departments that were subsidized by the fat and fixed commissions. If you were a star analyst, firms would gladly show you the money. Then they could pimp out your insights to those that did the most trades. No trades meant no information. When a salesman went to meet a top institutional account, they would bring an analyst along to help close the sale. There was nothing horrible about the system in many ways. If you had to pay the same amount, why not make Wall Street compete for the business?

There were problems. First, it was information to the highest trader, not bidder. Institutions were in a game of making trades to create the commissions necessary to get the research. This could cause some managers to trade more than they needed to pay for information. Second, it wasn't fair to the individual investor who simply didn't have the large sums of money to interest firms in letting loose the reports. Third, fixed commission rates were unfair. What if you did your own research and simply wanted to execute a trade? Why was it necessary for savvy investors to subsidize research departments if they did the research on their own? Furthermore, it hampered the independent research industry by keeping fees high and limiting the potential budget to buy from objective sources.

On one hand, the old school had some merits, but it gave the home-field advantage to the big players. The new system was supposed to change that, but you will see how it is the same game as before. With the Pay-Up Amendment in place, a money manager would not breach his fiduciary standard by paying a higher commission rate if that money manager in good faith determined the higher commission was worth it in relation to the research provided by the broker. This seems straightforward enough, other than the good faith part. Back then, regulators were more concerned about the best execution of trades, which was a serious issue before electronic trading allowed access to more liquidity when large blocks of shares had to be moved. But the big issue is simple: The benefit of paying more has to be for the client.

Soft Dollars

When fees were fixed, there was no real conflict of interest when a manager picked a brokerage firm as long as the execution of trades was at the best price available. This allowed the manager to explain to his clients that his advisory fees would include research purchased for the client's benefit. These were called soft dollars. While there were a few research services described above that could be purchased by hard dollars, or paid for by the adviser out of client fees, soft dollars came out of the client's pocketbook. Look at it this way: Fixed commissions made it easy for a money manager to keep more money by using soft dollars to pay for things instead of using his own money. The client was okay with this because they had no choice before May Day.

Now that commissions were negotiable, the money manager would have to justify, at least to regulators, that the higher fees brought value to the client. This was quite confusing considering the nature of soft dollars. You see, back then and still today brokerage firms add up the trades for the year then give you a budget of soft dollars to spend the following year. How can you measure what is benefiting a client over that span of time with tons of trades? You can't. Things got even crazier when many research departments started to get rid of their overhead. This was the start of independent research firms that would charge a fee for insight. Where would the money come from to fund it? Soft dollars. Eventually the SEC would allow brokerage firms to pay third-party research groups with money from the soft dollar accounts. This is tricky. You give a trade to a brokerage firm at a rate that is higher than the bare-bones, get-it-executed price. Then that brokerage firm essentially gives up the excess amount by paying a third party for research. This research is then given to the money manager for the benefit of the client. Sound confusing? Welcome to Wall Street.

In the real world this is how the system works, even today. Most individual investors that trade on their own don't think about how the system works. On a small level, let's look at how the Main Street investor is part of the soft dollar structure and doesn't even know it. Say you have two discount brokerage firms. One firm charges

$10 for a trade and the other charges $15. On the surface you may want to execute with the first brokerage and pay less. Then, after looking at the web sites and user interfaces, you come to the conclusion that the second, more expensive discount firm is the place for you. Why? Perhaps you liked the free research provided at no extra charge. Maybe you decided that access to fancier charting or trade management software was worth the extra money. All of this is a form of soft dollars, though not the way the SEC defines it. By choosing the firm that has the best services over the cheapest price, you are making a decision that the extra cost is to your benefit. Nobody would argue that this is a good thing, and with deregulated commissions it allows for a competitive market of discount brokerage providers. Our rigged system starts when your fiduciary money manager is making that decision, not you.

Think a fiduciary money manager is not something you have? Mutual fund managers and pension managers are fiduciary money managers. The term also includes managers that run portfolios for insurance companies that sell you annuity products. All of these managers have the ability to pay up and take soft dollars to buy things that they think will benefit you, but currently no system of auditing this exists. Sure, when the SEC comes in for an audit, they have a protocol of grilling the manager about soft dollars. The bottom line is that Section 28(e) gives a wide safe harbor with only a few guidelines and a lot of individual judgment to monitor it. After years of examination, the practice still exists. Now we are at a granular level of deciding if a subscription to the *Wall Street Journal* is a manager's overhead or research that can be paid for with soft dollars. It turns out it is not research since it is a mass-market publication, but a trade magazine about medical devices would qualify. Don't even get into the realm of technology and software programs.

In the end the practice will never end as long as commissions are negotiated. The only way to protect yourself is to do your own due diligence on the people that handle your money. Today the SEC requires a ton of disclosures so that if they miss the mark on finding all of the bugs, they at least warn you that a manager is making a decision on who gets the trade beyond best execution. The best advice to investors or a manger is to keep it simple. If you want to pay for things, do it yourself. If you use soft dollars or anything that resembles paying higher rates to get stuff, make sure that stuff is critical research that benefits the portfolio manager regardless of whether it's your money or someone else's.

Death of the Stockbrokers

After the massive shift in how individual investors bought stocks fueled by the electronic revolution of the Internet, Wall Street had to find a better way to get money out of clients. When you could trade a stock for $10, why pay a stockbroker? The industry wanted to get a piece of the action reserved for money managers and mutual funds. Specifically, by charging a fee on the assets under management (AUM). At issue were brokerage firms wanting to offer fee-based programs without having to be fiduciaries that only work in the client's best interests.

Why was this important? Under the Investment Advisers Act of 1940, people like me could register with the SEC and simply manage money. This means giving advice and trading for client's accounts. No commissions are taken from the adviser and no products are sold. It is simply advice for a fee. This essentially takes away the inherent conflicts of interest that arise when the person giving you advice is selling a security. By that very nature they don't always represent your best interests, but the interests of the brokerage firm. This is why a good stockbroker is hard to find and great ones simply don't exist. They usually end up on what we call the Registered Investment Adviser (RIA) side. Today there is little understanding of this distinction to the average consumer looking for advice. While there is much hype inside the industry, including champions of the fee-only model like the National Association of Personal Financial Advisors, it has never gained the attention it deserves. My take is that people ultimately don't care about ethics as long as the job gets done. However, isn't that what investors thought when Bernie Madoff offered a steady 10 percent return per year?

In 1999, the SEC started to look at proposals from brokerage firms to end fee-based brokerage programs. What was at stake was if broker-dealers—otherwise known as brokerage firms that hire stockbrokers—would be able to claim exemption under the Advisers Act of 1940. Specifically, brokers wanted to be exempt from the fiduciary standards that RIAs had to abide by, including always placing the client's interests ahead of his or her own. Making recommendations independent of outside influences is what an RIA is all about. Brokerage firms didn't have to do this at the time, and only needed to provide recommendations based on suitability, not the overall objective of the client's financial situation. This doesn't mean people hocking stock are bad, but they are not looking out for you as their primary motivator. All of this came to a head when brokerage firms argued that holding them up to the Advisers Act would impose a draconian and duplicative regulatory burden. I can see what they meant, but really? I find the rules for being an RIA are quite straightforward and less complicated than when I was on the other side of the fence as a broker. What was really happening was clients were flocking to discount brokerage firms to trade electronically at a lower commission rate. Something had to be done, or brokers would find themselves turned into a typewriter in the digital age.

To the chagrin of Wall Street, the SEC liked the idea of fee-based brokerage programs. It was simple; everybody at the time knew that working on commission induced brokers to churn accounts, which means buying and selling securities to generate commissions. I know what you could be thinking. Isn't turning people loose on electronic trading platforms letting them churn themselves? The SEC clearly didn't care, and still doesn't. Just look at High Frequency Traders that cause such a ruckus today. You can't tell me that allowing a *hedge fund* the ability to trade ten thousand times in under a second for a fat fee isn't churning.

Just because you didn't sell them the trade, you are selling them the power to generate commissions for the firm. Nothing wrong with it, but call it what it is without putting lipstick on it. In the end, Wall Street bullied the SEC into allowing the new programs under the concept that fee-based brokerage programs were simply re-priced

hedge fund   A private investment fund, it is different from mutual funds only in that a hedge fund can buy anything, be long or short, or use any type of leverage. Usually has a large part of the manager's money in it and comes with a performance fee on profits above the client's cost basis. Contrary to common beliefs, hedge funds are regulated, but simply have latitude on strategies employed. Like a car race, most people like to sit on the sidelines to see a crash, and don't bother learning the game.

commission structures and not really advice programs. Plus, if they didn't get the exception, they claimed the new programs would be scrapped. Score $1 trillion for Wall Street. This was a deal with the devil. In order to get brokers to stop churning accounts, the SEC allowed them to look like a fiduciary RIA. Proposal 202(a)(11)-1, also known as the Merrill Lynch rule, was put forth. It allowed the exemption of the fiduciary standard if the advice was non-discretionary, solely incidental to brokerage services, and fully disclosed. Practically speaking, it meant that the broker could walk and talk like a RIA, but still had to get permission to do the trades and figure out how to make the print fine enough in the disclosure to keep people from questioning them.

All hell broke loose. RIAs and financial planners were outraged that the perceived scumbag stockbrokers would now be allowed to wear sheep's clothing. A war was started between the lobbyist groups that represented brokers versus lobbying groups that represented the advisers. There was never a moment when either side wavered. Brokers claimed it was repricing of services, and advisers said any advice had to be under the Advisers Act. How did we get divided? Go back to the beginning of individual investing, which in the United States was born in the 1920s.

Short History of Advice

For hundreds of years, up until May Day 1975 when security commissions were deregulated, brokers gave advice as part of the fixed commission rate. This would go on for years and still does if you choose to pay a fat commission and trade through a traditional stockbroker. In the 1920s you didn't have stockbrokers or registered representatives as they are officially called today. Up until 1939 you dealt with customers' men. These guys were rainmakers that went out and got business. As your main point of contact, customers' men would get you information about tax shelters to stock reports. Because of the sales nature of the job, the stock exchanges didn't let them trade *discretionary accounts*.

In order to keep the sleaze away from true investment advice, firms started to develop their own internal departments designed to compete with independent consultants. It was here that the brokerage industry split up the concept of advising clients and acting on their behalf. One service of these new advisory departments

discretionary account   A managed account. This allows a broker or investment adviser to buy and sell securities without first receiving the client's consent. Most RIAs manage discretionary accounts, but it is rarely allowed for stockbrokers. This is also the litmus test to determine if a client actually wants a money management pro or simply wants to micromanage the account and have someone to bug.

was simply to give tips and suggestions, but the client would have to pull the trigger on the trade. This is no different than the fee-based brokerage programs firms use today, different only that back then you just paid the fixed commission. The second part was full discretionary management. Here the brokerage firm would have total control of trading securities on behalf of the client. It was expensive to get the service. Not only did you pay for AUM, but you also paid the same fixed commission mandated by the stock exchanges.

In the late 1930s Congress told the SEC to investigate this practice. In a 1940 report to Congress, the SEC suggested that there needed to be more regulation on so-called advisers who held themselves to a higher standard than just stock pickers. There would be registration requirements to separate the crackpots that held out to the public as investment counselors. From there the Advisers Act was created. Section 202(a)(11) defined an investment adviser as "any person who, for compensation, engages in the business of advising others, either directly or through publications or writings, as to the value of securities or as to the advisability of investing in, purchasing, or selling securities, or who, for compensation and as part of a regular business, issues or promulgates analyses or reports concerning securities."[1] This is the part that gets messy. Since Congress was looking at people who were not already regulated by the recently enacted Securities Act of 1933, they made an exception to the definition of "investment adviser" if a broker-dealer who provides the advice does so "solely incidental to the conduct of his business as a broker or dealer and who receives no special compensation therefor."[2] Thus, if you just take commissions and give out hot tips you are not really giving advice that needs to be regulated by a fiduciary standard. How is this helpful? It was prior to 1999 when commission brokers were clearly different in the way they got paid from investment advisers that charged on AUM. Any RIA could clearly state that they were paid directly from the client based on AUM, not a commission.

Fast forward to 1999 and this was turned on its head. Now broker-dealers were muscling in on the RIA business model, and with the SEC trying to curb churning, it allowed this travesty to happen. From that point forward, a common stockbroker could now call himself or herself an investment adviser, consultant, or the still-popular Vice President, and charge fees in a way that hides from the public the true nature of the business. This was not what Congress was trying to do back in 1940. It was clear that the Advisers Act was designed to separate advice that came about from selling stock for commission versus charging a fee on assets. Here is the problem. The SEC reasoned that Congress wrote the Advisers Act to include programs that included "special compensation,"[3] and at the time that really meant asset-based fees. Not only that, but the Advisers Act was really about regulating advisers that were not currently brokers under the 1933 Act. I get the point they make. Historically, brokers provide advice and other services to clients. Why then should they be held to another set of separate regulations just because they change how they charge their clients?

I suggest how you charge is not as important as the standard you live up to. Critics of the 1999 proposal, including myself, argue that the fiduciary standard 1940 Act advisers must hold themselves to would be denied to fee-based brokerage clients. After years of back-and-forth bickering, the SEC revamped the proposal. Rule 202(a)(11)-1(a) states that broker-dealers providing advice to clients are not required to treat them like advisory clients just because they charge on assets under management. All that is required is that the advice is solely incidental, meaning non-discretionary, and a big disclaimer to the client that this is a brokerage account and not an advisory account. Here is the language the SEC suggested:

"Your account is a brokerage account and not an advisory account. Our interests may not always be the same as yours. Please ask us questions to make sure you understand your rights and our obligations to you, including the extent of our obligations to disclose conflicts of interest and to act in your best interest. We are paid both by you and, sometimes, by people who compensate us based on what you buy. Therefore, our profits, and our salespersons' compensation, may vary by product and over time."[4]

Source: SEC Release Nos. 34-51523; IA-2376;
File No. S7-25-99, April 12, 2005.

Can we break this down? First, people outside the industry don't know what a brokerage or advisory account is. All accounts by nature are brokerage accounts. How else can you trade securities? When I was a broker, the thing people asked me right away when I sold these accounts was "Will you still advise me?" Of course, I said, I will always give you advice. What else could clients come up with after that? The next line says our interest may not be the same, and that the client should ask the broker questions. Then it tricks people who are not experts in legal language. It says "to act in your best interest." It doesn't say a broker won't, but simply you should ask what your rights are, and the broker's obligation to back them up. Nowhere in this disclaimer does it say the broker is not held to a fiduciary standard. The last line suggests that compensation may vary. Big deal, so now your client can sit around asking if you are getting paid more to offer certain funds over another. This is what happens. Instead of alerting people to the fundamental issue of working in the client's best interest, it directs the client to ask about how much money people are getting. This is how Wall Street rigs your relationships with the people who give you advice. The public knows that brokers want to get paid. Instead of addressing the fiduciary standard, in which an adviser can get paid to represent only the client's best interest, brokers just get people to ask if you get paid differently.

My point is simple. Even as advice has evolved into better structures than full commission brokerage schemes, people are still not addressing the standard of care they deserve. As soon as RIAs address the issue, brokerage firms rig the game so the public can't tell the difference. You see, even if brokers get the same pay to sell one stock or mutual fund over another, there is pressure to sell a whole lot more. Banking relationships, credit cards, mortgages, and insurance all become an opportunity for the firm to pressure their salespeople to increase revenue. Sure, there are investors and advisers that claim they are immune to such games. Unless the business structure is set up from the start to act in the client's best interest, how can you be sure it will always happen? You can't.

Avoiding Fleas

How can you as an investor protect yourself from the general confusion that the industry has created? Get on the same side of the table with your adviser. There will need to be a clear definition of what an adviser is. With the current state of regulation always changing, perhaps an expert who only acts in your best interest is a good start. It would be better to have this adviser barred from making any other choice. While it seems like a fairy tale to enforce ethics, it is not as hard as it sounds.

If you seek out an RIA firm that is open about how they make money, you are off to a good start. If the only form of compensation your money manager receives is the fees you pay him or her, you are on the right track. Does this mean that a person who makes money selling commission products is a horrible person? Not necessarily, but why take the chance if you don't need to? Sure, there are some very specific reasons why you would need to generate a commission for an adviser. Some of the top reasons include the sale of insurance for estate planning purposes. While I don't get involved in selling insurance directly, it is a normal part of high-end financial planning. In my experience, I see insurance products misused and improperly sold to unsuspecting investors. Insurance is a unique asset class since it is simply a contract with a corporation. After hundreds of years, there is still no way to access insurance products without generating a plain vanilla commission. This in no way means that you should never use them. But great care needs to be taken while selecting the person who is selling them to you.

If you have a long-term relationship with a so-called adviser, it is never too late to sit down and discuss his or her duty to you. It is not good enough to say that he or she is taking care of your interests. The adviser needs to be clear who they work for and what legal responsibility they have with managing your money. Often you will find that brokers are all too happy to explain that they are salespeople, but their job is to sell good stuff so you stay with them as a client. Hey, that would be an honest response! You get into a problem when they don't want to be clear on what they do.

4

Research by the Pound

Most people have lost sight of what a brokerage firm is really selling. Don't fret; I worked at a brokerage firm for four years before I was finally told. And this is after making a bundle of money! Needless to say I was shocked and a bit put off when told.

When I first got to Wall Street, my small firm said I could pitch any stock I wanted as long as it had a buy recommendation from any major brokerage house. I asked how to find out this information. After rolling their eyes at me, they walked me to a Bloomberg terminal.

Bloomberg terminals set the standard for financial information, especially bond prices, back in the 1980s. While they are still widely-used today in many brokerage firms, they won't really help the average investor. A monthly subscription costs almost $2,000, and unless you want to impress people, you can get your financial information somewhere else. My take is that these terminals can be a distraction and they can easily get you off your dime. If, on the other hand, you make your living trading bonds then you have to have one. In the end, they distract the professional the same way Wall Street distracts the average investor—too much *noise*!

noise Information encountered while researching markets that is irrelevant or fraudulent. To a trader, 99 percent of all news that the media and Internet produce is considered noise. When referring to brokerage-firm research reports, the noise can render the information in the report 100 percent useless.

upgrade or downgrade   Refers to a change in analyst ranking of a security or market. In practice, an upgrade is usually a signal of a top. Upgrading a stock allows the real players to sell their shares to latecomers who pile in like lemmings. When you are long a stock, you want an upgrade. Downgrades happen when a stock hits the bricks and the analyst wants to save face for recommending it. Both are generally useless unless you are trading in the short term, whereas most research is useless in both the short and long term.

Armed with this ultimate financial tool, I would type in the ticker symbol of the stock I wanted to buy and hit the required buttons. A list would be generated with all of the recent news associated with the company, along with various research reports. I was looking for *upgrades or downgrades.*

Sure, you could just go to the research report search, but how a company was being viewed by Wall Street was my main concern. Was a company being upgraded by other brokerage firms? Did anyone care? Was Wall Street as a whole hot for a company? All of this was contained by skimming the recent news stories. It wasn't necessary to read the reports; the first line on the screen was a *buy, sell, or hold recommendation,* followed by the name of the firm that wrote the report. Back then you needed the Bloomberg terminal. If any stock on that page had the word "buy" next to it, you were in business. It was the 1990s—every stock had a buy on it! If it had a sell, you can bet it wasn't a dot-com, and therefore nobody cared.

You can get the same information from any of the free financial sites available today. My favorite sites are still Yahoo! Finance and TheStreet.com. Yahoo! is just a basic place to get news feeds and a quote. It loads up quickly and lots of people use it. Why not observe what the crowd sees? Also, it is the best free site to look up historical prices, all the way back to 1962 in some cases. TheStreet.com is more for traders, so it is more geared to easy access to news that moves a stock, such as earnings announcements, economic numbers, and other traders' commentaries. I would find a financial web site that gives you the news you need, but keeps it simple enough to navigate. Too much information will leave you trapped online for hours.

Never in my short career as a stockbroker was I able to find a stock I wanted to buy that didn't have a buy recommendation from a major firm. I am sure these stocks existed, but I never came across one. It was not until I moved on to a larger brokerage firm

Buy, Sell, or Hold

While the words may seem straightforward, you have to read between the lines to fully understand the relationship between what is said and what you should do. When Wall Street says a stock is a buy, it usually means you should buy it. This is pretty clear. However, you then get into the vast array of qualifications of buy, strong buy, conviction buy, opportunistic buy, or bye-bye. A regular buy just means you can still own it if you have it already, and also allows your broker to sell it to you since it is approved for sale by their firm. A strong buy is a way of saying you should buy it right now, no questions asked, and purchase a lot of it. Conviction buy is a more sophisticated form of strong buy that usually has some fancy report that goes with it to show how clever the story is. Opportunistic buy means the stock is okay, but got blown up. It's so cheap, how could you not buy it? Bye-bye is when an institutional investor or trader sells their shares into the feeding frenzy that occurs after a buy recommendation. You can't sell a ton of shares unless a ton of people suddenly want to buy them.

Sell is a rare word on Wall Street. The dot-com crash led the government to put pressure on the industry to use the word in a context other than how to get people to open accounts. Investment bankers do not like when an analyst at their firm has a sell on a firm, since it is unlikely they will get investment-banking fees from them. Furthermore, a sell is hardly an optimistic word. It suggests that something exists that you should stay away from, like the plague or bird flu. Most often a sell is placed on a stock that is so dead and buried that nobody cares in the first place, but a firm selling research can get credit for a fair and balanced lineup of recommendations. It is kind of like affirmative action for stock ratings. The general trap for intrepid investors is letting the cynicism take over and looking for buys in the sell list. While I get the idea of looking for treasure in another person's trash, you are still fighting the tide. Sometimes it is better to just leave them alone. Plus, most of the time sells are really bad stocks!

Hold, by any other name, still means sell. Before firms had pressure to actually come out and say the word sell, they just said hold. Most of the time, a hold is explained to investors as a stock you shouldn't add to, but not sell either. This is rigged. You should always be careful with a hold rating. Why do you want to hold? Don't you want a strong buy? Did your strong conviction opportunistic buy become a hold? What makes it a hold now? You get the picture. When you own a stock that you consider a hold, it should either be getting near the point to take profits, or on a death watch. Be in or out, don't linger. If you are in a stock for the long run, these ratings should not make any difference to your decision-making process. Thus, if you dare to care about ratings like buy, sell, or hold just watch the first one and leave the last two in the dust.

that did its own research that I figured out what was happening. When you are a stockbroker, you are selling securities. These securities have to pass some level of due diligence by the firm you work for. When I was at the small shop, we didn't have a formal research department, so we were simply told that the outside research we received was good enough for us. Frankly, this was honest, and I was not beholden to one firm's garbage—I had the whole dump to pick through. And yes, the industry also self-regulates the research, with no outside oversight before publishing the information. This ensures we have the home field advantage all the time.

So, although it seemed easy enough to get a hold of research, it was not helpful, nor did it lead me in any direction. There were plenty of people on the trading floor of the firm I worked for with sales pitches that appeared to work. Why not just pick up on what the other guys were doing, since some big place already did the work for us, right? It was when I moved to Bear Stearns, a major firm with its own research department, that I finally got the big picture. (Yes, *that* Bear Stearns.) During my first day on the job I was greeted by a visit from my new manager. "What are you pitching?" he asked me. I told him some ticker symbol that had a good story and was working to open new accounts.

His response was stone cold. "Where is the firm's research report?" My blank stare betrayed my ignorance of the question. He said, "No, no way, you are here to do one thing—sell Bear Stearns research." I was floored. Nobody had ever explained the basis for my existence so clearly before. Was this it? Was my sole reason for existence just to resell a buy, sell, or hold recommendation by an analyst I would never meet? At least the analyst was in the same building and worked for my firm. But wait, wasn't this worse than before? When I started out I could do my own work and take the

story The bread and butter of stockbrokers and analysts. A story refers to a series of persuasive data points that, if presented in the right manner, will induce a reasonable person to ignore proper due diligence and buy a stock on emotion. Story is used to create the immediate need to buy or sell the security without delay. A good story will make you trade now. A bad story will cause you to think long enough to pass. Stories may utilize rumors, statistics, charts, alcohol, and box seats at New York Knicks games.

best of what was out there. Granted, I had little to no training, but it forced me to teach myself. I was not born yesterday, and could see there was a clear connection between what the analysts said and how that was going to affect the investment banking business of the firm.

Big investment banking firms make money raising capital for corporations, merging those corporations, and getting those corporations to buy other corporations. Other services can include selling stock to investors directly. You can't raise capital in the form of stock if you have nobody to sell it to. From a very simple perspective, these firms find companies to take public, get their brokers to find investors willing to buy the stock, and pass along that money to the now public company minus the pound of flesh we call investment banking fees. Wouldn't it be a nice touch if those firms had good things to say about the publicly traded companies they were trying to get business from? I would say yes, but the regulators say that would be a conflict of interest. After the crash of 1929, the government realized that it would be a good idea to separate the inside knowledge of investment banking from the sales force in a vain attempt to make things fair for investors. Thus, there is an imaginary thing called a Chinese Wall. A Chinese Wall means that there is an invisible wall that separates the dealmakers from the share buyers. Please don't ask me if this is politically correct or not—nobody on Wall Street cares about walls that are constructed in China. This is actually a compliment to the Chinese, because it suggests that they can make invisible walls that actually work! And maybe this is accurate, since China can control the news and media inside their country, whereas Wall Street is not that talented. What we have is a situation in which one company provides both information to the public, or sell-side analysts, and information for specific firms and mutual funds, or buy-side analysts. In the end it is simply a game of cat and mouse between Wall Street and regulators.

There was a huge crackdown on this behavior after the tech crash of 2000. The core issue was very specific. Firms were putting out buy recommendations on companies they knew were going down the tubes. Internal e-mails at several firms proved that many people inside certain firms were complaining about this practice. I remember a heated conversation with a stockbroker back at Bear Stearns asking how their analyst still had a $200 price target on an Internet stock trading at less than $20. Sadly, all he wanted was a new, realistic, and lower price target because his clients were questioning the competence of the firm. The crackdown came in the form of an enforcement agreement called the Global Settlement of 2003. The SEC, National Association of Securities Dealers, the New York Stock Exchange Regulation (the NASD and NYSE Regulation combined to become FINRA in 2007), and 10 top investment firms came together to reach a compromise. This agreement was created to address conflicts of interest within the largest investments firms. In a nutshell, the parties involved were trying to address the conflicts of publishing research reports that told people what to buy or sell when they also were involved in investment banking business. It's like saying you will create the product and judge if people should buy it or not. While most people working on Wall Street are clearly aware when one firm is promoting and researching the same stock, Main Street trusted that the industry had checks and balances. All they got was the Chinese Wall. As a result, 10 large firms were clipped for a total of $1.45 billion in fines. It was a simple case of issuing fraudulent research reports, exaggerating claims about companies, getting paid for research reports and not telling investors, and giving hot initial public offerings (IPOs) to company executives. Don't laugh, the government really thought they were cleaning up Wall Street, and Wall Street didn't want them to think differently. Two guys were chosen to fall on the sword: Jack Grubman and Henry Blodget.

These were no ordinary patsies. Jack Grubman was the poster boy for the dot-com crash. He was infamous for putting out positive reports on the now-bankrupt Global Crossing and WorldCom. A superstar telecom analyst, he worked at Salomon Smith Barney at the time. His big buildup was in 2000 when he told *Business Week* "What used to be a conflict is now a synergy."[1] And don't tell him about a Chinese Wall. "Objective? The other word for it is uninformed." The best thing he ever did to earn the top spot on the sleaze list was the e-mail to one of his friends in 2002 regarding his motivation to change a stock recommendation:

> "You know everyone thinks I upgraded [AT&T] to get lead for [AT&T Wireless]. Nope. I used Sandy to get my kids in 92nd ST Y pre-school (which is harder than Harvard) and Sandy needed Armstrong's vote on our board to nuke Reed in showdown. Once coast was clear for both of us (ie Sandy clear victor and my kids confirmed) I went back to my normal negative self on [AT&T]. Armstrong never knew that we both (Sandy and I) played him like a fiddle."[2]

You can find the original memo Grubman wrote to Sandy Weill (head of Citigroup, which owned Salomon Smith Barney at the time) that outlines the gory details, if you are still up for it.[3] Needless to say he was busted by then-Attorney General Elliot Spitzer, banned from the securities industry for life, and ordered to pay a $15 million fine. It was still good business for Grubman. After getting a $30 million severance package, he went on to work for the Magee Group. His new firm provides strategic consulting for telecom and technology companies, just no IPOs or investment banking this time around.[4]

Henry Blodget had a different approach than moving around opinions just to get kids into a top preschool. Blodget was all about stocks going in one direction. He made his name by saying that Amazon.com shares would go to $400. It happened. Then Merrill Lynch hired him and he became the top analyst of the era. At a time when most dot-com stocks were going up, he was the main cheerleader. If you made money getting Internet firms to go public, which Merrill Lynch was doing at the time, Blodget was the guy to hire. With his track record of eternal optimism, any firm going public with Merrill knew they were going to get a stellar score from the research department. Then came the crash, Elliott Spitzer, and some truly memorable e-mail that ended with Blodget being banned from the securities industry for life. On the same day Merrill Lynch gave Excite (ticker ATHM at the time) their second highest rating, Blodget sent an internal e-mail saying "ATHM is such a piece of crap!"[5] The same thing happened for Lifeminders (Does anybody remember this company?) when Blodget e-mailed his internal assessment stating "I can't believe what a POS that thing is." No, that is not some special Wall Street code for particularly outstanding stock. POS is universal. At least we got some insight as to why this was happening, with the e-mail explaining "This company [InfoSpace] is very important to us from a banking perspective, in addition to our institutional franchise."

I find it hard to believe anyone would do business with Merrill Lynch from that point on. At least now the firm proved they couldn't be trusted with anything, including its own checkbook. In 2008, amid the financial crisis, Bank of America picked up the Merrill Lynch "POS." The mortgage crisis got the best of Merrill and they had to merge or die. Greed and bad decisions apparently will catch up with you. Well, not really. Merrill Lynch is still taking money from its clients, and as for Blodget, he is still talking. Blodget has a new career covering financial news, starting with articles about the Martha Stewart insider trading trial. Next came a series of articles about the general sickness of Wall Street. Today Blodget is CEO and Editor-In-Chief of Internet web site Business Insider— they have even written articles about me! You have to stop and give this guy some credit. Sure, he should be in jail because he knew what he was doing was corrupt. While he paid a $4 million fine he is far from having practical banishment from the industry. He can still buy and sell for his own account, and can advise members of the general public on what they should do with their money. Next time you watch TechTicker on Yahoo!, an online video show, look at the host. America is clearly tolerant of second acts, even when fraud is involved.

The bottom line is that when you get a recommendation from a brokerage firm, it doesn't matter if you are a hedge fund manager or a retail investor. They are selling you the output of an analyst who is paid by the pound. You lose from the very beginning. While I have explained how you can get misled by this practice, now let's find out why we all fall into the trap.

Research by the Pound

At the beginning of every year a new set of games and diversions start on Wall Street in some of the largest investment firms in order to keep you on a steady diet of nothing. The preparations begin in September when new recruits start arriving in Manhattan to fill the empty desks of prior analysts. After a year or two there is an exodus of young analysts that, either by choice or force, go back to school to accumulate more debt. Someone has to fill the seats once school is back in session. A ton of money and time is spent by these firms for the main purpose of keeping investors from asking the right questions. Useless drivel spouts from a new cast of starry-eyed kids straight out of college, and around two years later they leave the business in disgust or go back to get an MBA in order to continue their careers as analysts. It's time for the annual running of bull, the beginning-of-the-year prognostication reports. You may not recognize these reports as an annual event, but Wall Street works on a calendar just like the rest of the world. The industry needs big ideas to sell to Main Street, and a broad overview of what happened the year before and what is expected going forward happens in January. Plus, this is when investors get their annual statements. If they are not happy with the performance, this is the time when market share can be taken simply by having a viewpoint that is different from a competitor that posted lousy annual numbers for their clients.

These reports are created by firms that want you to trade with them. Anywhere from Barclays to Goldman Sachs will produce them. Also, there are smaller boutique firms that have a specialty such as bank stocks or government bonds. Ultimately anyone can print this stuff, but the main differentiating factor is the ability to monetize the information with commissions. Understanding the big picture is the first layer that will tell you where and how a firm sees the world. These are the *global macro* reports that go over how the world is supposed to turn, with a special emphasis on political trends, long-term economic trends, and the wildcards that could come out and bite you.

For me, this is the most interesting stuff because there is an attempt to pull all markets together and make sense of them all. If you play four-dimensional chess games, this is your junk food. While easy to read, it is bad for your health. I do find some value in understanding other markets and how they have performed over the past year. Also, the big overviews will give you the general sense of what a firm's attitudes or biases of certain markets are. For instance, if a major firm has a poor view on stocks from the high level, you can't get that excited about their top stock picks. If, on the other hand, they think commodities can't be stopped that year, how critical will they be when differentiating cotton from copper?

From here we get into each of the desks and their markets. At big firms, a desk is used to describe a particular group that trades

global macro   Generally defined as a management style using world economic data to formulate investment decisions. In practice this is what traders say when they want to be the big man on campus. In practice, a global macro trader uses the largest indexes of stocks, bonds, and commodities, taking long and short positions. Examples include the S&P 500, 10-year U.S. Treasury bonds, oil, and currency. It is considered more respectable to be a global macro trader than a degenerate small-cap stock jock. I, of course, trade global macro and will never go back.

specific markets. One desk could just be government securities and another could be emerging market stocks. Most will have a few analysts that comment on what they see as the top opportunities to make money. Don't forget that they are selling trades. If you read a great idea, you are supposed to call them up and tell them to load up your truck. One thing that I like to do is read about another market that I don't trade. The classic example is reading bond traders' analysis on companies when researching to buy the stock. Bond traders are concerned about a company being able to pay their bills and keep a good credit rating. If something is flaring up, the bond traders will see the smoke first. Of course, there are many stocks that came back from the dead long after the bond traders moved on. Also, I have been a fan of looking at currency prognostications. While most of it can change direction faster than a Fed meeting, if one country's currency is favored above another country's currency, that country's bond and stock market will be close behind it.

Most of these reports are for professional investors looking for trading ideas. If you are not a professional investor who is used to the incredible amount of information available, it can get you off your dime. In the end, if you are using these research reports to find something to buy, you are in trouble. Before you open the pages, you need to know what your plan is. In other words, don't go to the supermarket hungry. If my hedge fund is thinking about changing what markets we trade, it could be helpful to see the outlook. A volatile year could mean more trading opportunities than a part of the market expected to be flat. You're looking for action, not necessarily what the analyst is suggesting you do.

Come on, I love to read these reports. Why think for yourself when a stack of papers is at hand that tells you the best places to put your money for the next 12 months? Every report is the same, yet just different enough for you to lay them out and decide what to pick and choose from. We on the institutional side are even more entranced, because there exists a special version of these reports that are not for public consumption that comes out late in the prior year. Under the heading of institutional research, professionals can get more candid information. This is partly because of lighter regulation for information given to a financial professional versus what is given to the general public. Due to regulation that is intended to protect regular investors, firms' internal compliance departments simply do not allow some information to be let loose.

Unfortunately, this creates a two-tier system just because a bunch of attorneys have to be overly involved with what can go out to nonprofessionals.

What are you missing? It is hard to say. I find that the main issue is simply suitability. You can't talk about trading currency to most individual investors, and that goes for commodities as well. Most of that stuff is considered unsuitable for people who are not considered accredited investors with a net worth of a million dollars or making more than $200,000 per year. The rule was designed to protect people from using their rent money on hot tips, but there are plenty of suckers with a million bucks to lose. Certain strategies that might be suggested for hedge fund managers are not appropriate for Main Street investors. For instance, institutional research might suggest a buy on one stock with a *short* on another. Generally, a firm will not recommend shorting stock to retail investors. As a Main Street investor, you will get less research, less commentary from the analysts, and less information about other markets.

As a cycle, most of these reports will not be floating around by the end of the year. Things change, and who wants a bad call sitting on your desk reminding you how wrong you were? Most of these reports will have several updates and revisions by the summer months. Fall is another big rush, as professionals, like everyday workers, come back from summer vacation and try to grind out some profits by the winter holidays. Let's follow the trail on who uses what report and how it gets down to your doorstep.

The Report Trail

Research has only one purpose—to sell brokerage services. This is called sell-side research. It exists so that salespeople can solicit

short Generally used to describe selling a security short. This is done by borrowing the security from a brokerage firm, then selling it with the hope of buying it back cheaper. Also known as the way to blow up a hedge fund since you have unlimited loss versus a long position that can only go to zero. Describes intestinal distress during market surges, that is, "I'm short the market." Also used to gloat when a trader has sold a security and it tanks, that is, "I'm short Enron." Designed to allow traders to make money in all market conditions, generally it leads to short-term memory loss and poor marital relations.

trades from hedge funds, institutional investors, and the retail public. Firms on the sell-side get money every time a security is traded, so you can see how provocative research that induces a trade is good for business. By luring in the investors, no matter who they are, Wall Street can get their trades and make money. This is why you need to be a client of a firm before you get their secret picks for the year. Now, this does not include things like newsletters, which you pay the writer for directly. Why? Because people that write newsletters don't own a brokerage firm! I do have a few favorite newsletters that I still get. Tom McClellan has an excellent daily service that covers the technical aspects of the market. Also Helene Meisler's *Top Stocks* is available from TheStreet.com and provides ideas for trading stocks using charts. However, reducing your sources is essential to success. As you get better at playing the game, you choose to read some people even though you don't trade what they trade. You simply want to hear their side of the story. I find value in hearing other traders' ideas even if I disagree with them or have a different style of trading. These folks make money only if you pay them for the information. I like this better because I know there is no ulterior motive. These sources are also for the most part single individuals versus a large group compiled to create sell-side propaganda. A herd of young analysts are sent on a mission to find new facts about companies and challenge the current recommendations, not for any type of intellectual pursuit, but to mix things up and create more activity. While high-frequency trading is making this research less attractive, there will always be a need to feed the beast.

From the top, you start with hedge funds. Remember that a hedge fund is just a private partnership of wealthy investors or institutions run by a money manager. Hedge funds are still regulated, but have huge latitude with what they can buy or sell. They tend to trade faster and with leverage—meaning they are more valuable than other types of brokerage clients. Most have zero loyalty to any firm and do what is called *trade aways*. This means the hedge fund usually has a main broker that holds its securities (known in the business as a prime broker), but will do a trade outside that firm if the fund likes the idea. Stop and think about this for a moment. A hedge fund is being sold trades by every firm that can pitch it an idea. If the portfolio manager likes the idea, the trade is done through that firm, usually at a slightly higher commission rate than their prime broker. It goes like this:

"Hey, Lee, it's Rick over at Long Island Securities. We are an institutional research house specializing in banking stocks" (It can be anything, but mostly they say they do something in particular).

"Our top analyst has a strong buy on XYZ Company and earnings are coming out tomorrow. We think it will go higher."

At this point they will want to send the portfolio manager their report, get a big share order for the hedge fund, and charge around five cents a share versus the one to two cents that your prime broker charges. If you do the trade, your back office arranges delivery of the shares to your prime broker. It's like ordering something on Amazon.com and three days later it comes to your house. Get the picture? These places need a constant stream of garbage to make pitches to hedge funds. The money is in the trades. The report is rigged, because there is zero reason for a long-term investor to read it. It's not designed to do anything but create a story with a catalyst, real or imagined. The classic reports are about being long or short based on a better or worse quarterly earning announcement. If you read this you are simply looking for what we call *idea flow*. This is a fancy way of saying you need something to trade or are bored.

The good news is that you don't have to worry about the follow up. The institutional sales trader will eventually call back to sell out the shares at a loss or gloat about the profit. The insult to injury is that they will always ask you, "What do you want to do?" as if you are the one that came up with the idea. This is how they keep you from focusing on making money. Instead of guiding you through a trade and taking responsibility, they get you in the position, then reinforce that you made the decision based on their research. Remember, brokers, institutional or not, don't provide advice, they are just pimping out the research.

Not everyone buys into this, and I have had my turn at sales traders. Now I just stick to my own strategies and keep the wolves at bay. Don't cry for them. My prime broker makes plenty of pennies off of me.

An institutional investor is the next rung looking for a fix. This can be a pension fund, mutual fund, or maybe an insurance company. There are other perks that come with working with the sell-side. Some institutional investors will have access to firm-sponsored IPOs or other new securities not offered to non-clients. Looking for that hard-to-get muni-bond offering? How many trades have you done with us lately? If you are light on attention span, an expensive dinner or sporting event is just the thing to focus your mind. In the end, this creates a slippery slope. Can you remain objective if your sales rep is always showering you with this type of attention?

We see this behavior go all the way down to Main Street, USA. By now it is obvious that the green fees paid for by the stockbroker are coming out of your commissions. In the end we know this, or at least try to ignore it. Some places do provide good research. The problem is that it mostly comes from other hedge funds and portfolio managers. Often professionals will pass around their work. This is information the public never sees. Most individual investors do not have the background to decipher or even identify top work. If you understand what the game is, you can beat it. However, I find that this is a game best left alone. Wall Street is offering advice on a question you didn't ask. Great gossip, but know to toss it in the stack next to the tabloids.

CHAPTER 5

401(k): Gun to Your Head

On April 18, 1906, an earthquake hit San Francisco, burning most of the city to the ground. Telephone and telegraph lines were destroyed, temporarily cutting off communication with the rest of the country, especially Wall Street. Eight days later, the New York Stock Exchange (NYSE) had lost a billion dollars or 12.5 percent of market value. It took a week for investors and speculators to figure out how to play the disaster. The knee-jerk reaction to the economic impact was like slow motion compared to the crash of 1929, which had the benefit of radio to broadcast the panic on a daily basis. You can understand how things have changed since then. Back then you couldn't use your smart phone to take a picture of your house burning down or tweet about the destruction of San Francisco to your friends. Today, the world knew immediately about the 20-minute long Flash Crash of May 6, 2010, and was able to watch the market recover in real time. Is it progress that we are now at the point of 20-minute long stock market crashes? Technology has created a false veneer of total information awareness. I'm here to expose how a few specific events occurred that contributed to the delinquency of the long-term investor.

Many market prognosticators like to spit out factoids of how the average holding period of stocks back in the 1950s was around eight years. Today it is around six months (Figure 5.1). Clearly, over the past 60 years we as a society have become traders. We have no idea why this occurred. Were people that into Elvis and hot rods that they didn't trade their accounts? Did they just forget? This chapter

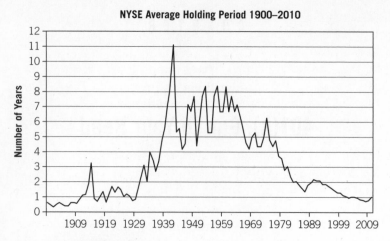

Figure 5.1   Stone Age Day Traders

Source: http://www.nyxdata.com/factbook

explores three particular factors that I believe contributed to this decline in long-term holding patterns. Before we delve into things, it should be noted that the world didn't start in the 1950s. In fact, the average holding period of stocks was well under two years from 1900 all the way until the 1930s. What does this mean? Perhaps we were always traders. I just want to know how we got back to our natural state. What made us come full circle? There are a number of reasons, including being forced to invest for retirement versus having a pension, easy access to trading mutual funds that in turn trade the markets, and converting stock pushers into fund pushers.

How We Became Traders

What happened in the 1980s aside from crappy cars and awesome hairstyles? Congress unknowingly put a gun to the head of the American worker. You want to blame evil corporate CEOs for killing pension plans? Go ahead, but until there were laws allowing them to do it, their greedy hands were tied. We need to understand how the individual investor started to increase his or her exposure to stocks in record numbers. While the 1920s put stocks on the map for their speculative qualities and wealth-building promise, it wasn't until the 1980s that the public was forced to invest.

First, how did we get here? Remember the good old days when you worked for a company and part of your pay automatically went into a pension? I don't. It really was a great idea, but when I was three years old Congress put a single line in the Revenue Act of 1978 under section 401(k). The main line was: "under which a covered employee may elect to have the employer make payments as contributions to a trust under the plan on behalf of the employee." That was it. In plain English, this was designed to allow a company to put money into a tax-deferred investment plan. However, the difference was this money was not based on the future benefit or payout of the plan. That is how a pension works, by setting aside money now for a specific benefit in the future, like 50 percent or 100 percent of your current salary. This is what teachers and other public workers that are lucky enough to be outside the real world are talking about when they rattle off how many years before they get some percentage of their compensation paid to them for life. Now you can understand why they're sensitive about how long people should have to work before getting a guaranteed income stream at retirement. The 401(k) was all about putting money aside without the obligation of a guaranteed income stream. It was just cash in an account, period. From the point of view of the corporation, they would no longer have a future liability to fund those workers. Think of the challenges General Motors had when they were paying pension benefits for retired workers. Because they ran an inefficient business with horrible products, the added stress of benefits they had to pay to pensioners became too much. GM had to declare bankruptcy and start over.

By 1979, Johnson & Johnson had begun the process of adopting a 401(k), and the U.S. worker has been riddled by noise ever since. What an outrage! All those cute babies from the No Tears baby shampoo commercials now with parents that had to save for their own retirement with no secure income stream. I say let those babies cry. It only took a few years for other corporations to figure out what this meant. They could drop expensive pension plans in which they were required to make good on a benefit, and shift the burden to the employee. Why not? Well for one thing, it's irresponsible. Most people have no education on how to invest like a pro. Without the oversight of a professional *pension manager* who can calculate how much to save, how to invest capital, and what amounts to distribute 30 years from now, there was little hope of success. Most plans do little more than provide a meaningless list of mutual funds that few people know anything about.

pension manager   Someone has to do it. A pension is simply an arrangement or promise to pay an employee money once he or she is no longer working. This money is set aside over the employee's lifetime and invested by a professional manager. The manager must also manage the current and future liabilities of the pensioners, not simply grow the money. In this way, the aim of the manager may not be for growth as much as the certainty that money will be available for payout at a future date based on a known formula, usually based on a worker's salary. State and municipal pensions seem to have a magic formula since most are currently underfunded. It is rumored that taxpayers will for some reason want to pitch in and pay for public workers' retirements. In the private sector, a corporation can simply file for bankruptcy and the government will bail out the pension.

This was the moment the mutual fund industry was hoping for: A legitimate reason for the Main Street investor to be forced to buy their products. It was like making everyone drive a car, brilliant! To add to the mess, after a few decades of the 401(k) as the replacement for a pension, the average worker began to look at it as some type of benefit. To be fair, it is a benefit to the mutual fund industry and its salespeople. In order to keep up the pace, it would have to be expanded to almost everyone. Walk a mile in the shoes of a small business owner to understand how the culture of the 401(k) has overtaken logic.

Small business owners are preyed upon by everyone from people pretending they are from your phone company trying to sell you cheap long distance to those peddling employee benefits. You know the drill. A trusted adviser tells you it is necessary to set up a 401(k) or you won't be able to attract top talent. Before jumping into a retirement plan that is expensive, complicated, and burdened by compliance demands, small business owners need to ask, why bother? Some think it is a good way to provide for an employee's retirement, and others think of it as a benefit needed to compete for talent with another company down the street. Maybe that is the problem. You never started the plan to help your people replace their income in the future; you were *sold* the plan as an employee benefit. Sorry, health care is a benefit, but a 401(k) is a whole other beast. With most of the new jobs created in this country originating from small businesses, we have a systemic problem on our hands.

A 401(k) for a small business does nothing but entrap the company into a lot of fees, confusion, and, at worst, a clumsy way for employees to waste time. A 401(k) is comprised of four groups: a third-party administrator (TPA), custodian, record keeper, and investment manager. They're all taking your money just so you can put a little away and save some taxes. That doesn't even cover a slick salesperson.

Don't get me wrong, if you run a large corporation you can afford the economies of scale and groupthink of a 401(k) plan. Big companies attract those that want protection from boutique firms specializing in free thought. However, if you really wanted to attract talent at a big firm, why not start pensions up again? Teachers love their jobs and don't want to leave! But as the owner of a small business, you have other options. Learn about the alternatives; a Simplified Employee Pension (SEP) IRA, Savings Incentive Match Plan for Employee (SIMPLE) IRA, and all forms of pension trusts may be a better fit. A SIMPLE or SEP IRA is easy to set up and virtually free. Your bookkeeper or certified public accountant (CPA) can do the calculation or you can even do it yourself. A pension trust may be more appropriate for a smaller firm with highly paid employees such as doctors and lawyers. The trusts can be a single account, managed by a professional (you have a little more bargaining power to get a real manager with a larger account than you do with a bunch of tiny ones), and a third party administrator (TPA) can do the accounting once a year. The more professional management you can offer your employees, the more it will become a benefit. Do you really want your employees making these decisions themselves?

If you are lucky enough to provide other people with employment, do them a service, a real benefit, and do no harm. Would you issue an employee a gun to keep them safe? Police are issued guns, but receive years of ongoing training to use them correctly. When they use them incorrectly, the public gets really upset. When was the last time that there was a protest about a cubicle worker blowing up his or her retirement account by *day trading*?

It should come as no surprise that the police are given a pension plan that is managed by trained professionals. This gives them more time to stop me from speeding versus trading their 401(k). My point is simple. Giving people an investment vehicle with no real training is like giving them a loaded weapon. Being the boss

day trading   A commonly misunderstood term for anybody who trades a lot; a day trader is a speculator who buys and sells a security during the same day. Often used as a criticism by those who wish life could be as simple as buy and hope towards investors who use risk management to protect capital. Can be used to describe your next-door neighbor who lost his job and is now in the process of blowing up his finances by trading his IRA all day instead of looking for work.

sometimes means leading people, and the first place to start is financial literacy. If you are not the boss, act like one and demand more.

The bottom line is that Americans are gambling with their retirements and the government forced it on them. By creating the 401(k), the government was able to get rid of pensions, rigging a system where uneducated investors are forced to compete with professional traders against their will. Sure, mutual funds help, but not if you are in a captive environment with little choice as to the quality and flexibility that free access to all markets provide. People lack the education to understand how much they will need to save and invest in order to retire. Putting these two ideas together explains a lot when looking at a baby boomer population that has nothing to retire on.

The Mutual Fund Supermarket Is Born

Once Congress allowed Wall Street to put us on a forced diet of mutual funds, it was only a matter of time before the system of buying and selling funds was taken to a whole other level. Remember the old days? I don't. Back in the 1980s buying a mutual fund was a complete pain in the neck. You had to write a check to the fund company, mail it, call the fund company to place instructions, and don't even thing about moving money around during a market crisis (or opportunity). If you used a broker to do this, large commissions in the form of a load came out of your initial investment, not to mention ongoing trials referred to as *12b-1 fees*.

It was not as if fund companies were trying to make things hard for you, it was just that there was a lack of technology. It didn't help that they were looking for the money to go only one direction—they

12b-1 fees   According to the Securities and Exchange Commission (SEC), these are distribution fees paid by a mutual fund for marketing and selling fund shares. This includes advertising, printing and mailing sales literature, and sending out prospectuses. Most importantly it is payment to brokers who push the funds. 12b-1 is a reference to the rule that authorizes the payments directly to the broker that marketed the fund to you. Also, if no actual broker sold it to you, the discount brokerage firm that did the transaction keeps the money. This is why you can trade some funds for free online, and others have a fee. You have to pay one way or another.

got paid the longer you were in the funds. In 1984 Charles Schwab came up with a great idea called the Mutual Fund MarketPlace. According the company web site, it started out with 140 no-load funds. You still had to pay a small fee to buy or sell, but it was a lot easier, considering that you could have multiple funds under one account. Basically, it meant that you could run a mutual fund portfolio the same way that a stock account ran. Instead of having each fund held directly, you simply consolidated your funds inside a brokerage account. This was like having stocks in a single account versus holding individual certificates in a safety deposit box. It was not until 1992 that the offensive stuff started to happen. OneSource was created to make "mutual funds easier, less expensive and accessible to all."[1] Schwab says this with a straight face. With more than $8 billion coming into the program the first year, I would keep a straight face too. Yes, it was an innovation—about how to blackmail mutual funds to buy shelf space and pass the cost to the end user. You know, the people that Uncle Chuck is trying to help. I would be less harsh if it were not for the populist attitude that the company has taken in its marketing campaigns over the years.

Let me break down how this so-called free lunch of buy-whatever-fund-you-want-with-no-fee actually works. And for full disclosure, most firms do this, but since Schwab was the innovator of the fee farm, he should get first dibs on the commentary.

In order to keep this simple, we are going to break things down into two categories: Funds that have no transaction fee versus funds that charge a fee to transact. In the business, we call the first type NTFs, or no-transaction-fee funds. Some so-called advisers love this because they can charge you 1.5 percent a year to manage mutual funds, buy NTFs, and you never see any commissions or transactions. If you asked the manager to buy you institutional class shares, you would start to see fees every time the adviser made any type of trade. It is one thing if you are working with a small account where transaction fees can add up, but above the $25,000 to $50,000 range, those fees start to impact performance.

NTFs (11,300 on Schwab's platform) pay about 0.4 percent of the assets held at the firm, not to mention the $10,000 fee just to get a fund on the platform. Yes, you heard me right. Schwab charges the mutual fund that you just bought at no charge around 0.4 percent just to have the right to be on the shelf. How is this different that a supermarket that charges a product for shelf space? It's not. I think it is gross, because it increases the cost to the investor. On Schwab's own web site they clearly state, "To the extent that any part of these fees is paid out of fund assets, fees are included in the fund's operating expense ratio (OER), which means the fees are indirectly borne by the fund's shareholders."[2]

Wow, fees are borne by the fund's shareholders—which in English means you eat the pay-to-play arrangement and the mutual fund gets to hide it deep in the bowels of its operating expenses. Then you want to yell at the high expenses of funds? To be fair, it is the fund manager that signed the deal with the devil. With all of the new funds added to the universe over the past 20 years, companies will do anything for an edge, even if it means paying up so you can buy the fund at no charge. There have also been high-profile cases where the managers said no dice. Longleaf Partners got fed up back in 2003 when Schwab raised the OneSource fees to 40 basis points. In a letter to shareholders, the fund said that the fees were "duplicative and excessive."[3] Schwab shot back and prohibited clients from purchasing Longleaf funds except for a select group of institutional advisers. The only problem is that Schwab decides who gets to be a part of that select group. Now that doesn't sound fair to me.

Big players with their own marketing muscle like Vanguard and American Funds would rather be out of the NTF game. How could Vanguard offer rock bottom prices if forced to pay 0.4 percent to Schwab? Well, they just pay less. That is easy to do if you are already a major player with strong demand.

If you are using a transaction fee fund—the type of fund where you pay a small fee to trade in your brokerage account—Schwab still gets some money from the fund. Schwab says it is usually $20, but "sometimes as high as $30." Oh boy, I hope I don't end up starting a mutual fund or Chuck will definitely charge *me* $30 if he even lets me in his club at all. But, they go on to say some funds choose to pay up to 0.25 percent on assets held at Schwab. Now, don't forget the $10,000 one-time establishment fee. To add insult to injury, "Both types of fees *are in addition to the transaction fee that shareholders pay to Schwab.* There are approximately 3,175 fee funds available for Schwab clients to choose from. [emphasis added]"[4]

So, if we accept that Schwab has to make a lot of money, just like any self-respecting Wall Street pirate, is there any real harm in it? A little bit. After you get beyond the higher prices that Schwab forces funds to pay (the fund still chooses this route versus a possibly more expense alternative marketing approach), you get to how Schwab recommends funds. This is where the system is rigged.

When you do business with a discount brokerage firm, they try to show you all the ways their web site can help you make informed decisions. You know, do it on your own versus taking the bad advice of a pro. Hey, if Home Depot says you can do it, Schwab also wants to help. When looking at mutual funds you will first find that there are more funds than stocks on the NYSE. The answer, according to Uncle Chuck: "With thousands of mutual funds available, finding the right funds for your portfolio can seem more time-consuming and difficult than ever. The Mutual Fund OneSource Select List, consisting only of OneSource funds available without a load or transaction fee, is a smart solution that can help you make confident investment decisions."[5]

Thank goodness there is a smart solution, because I was not looking for stupid. Add some confidence and the comfort that these funds are available without an evil load or horrible transaction fee and we are out of the woods. Yet, as you go all the way down to the bottom of the disclaimer of the OneSource Select List, in plain English it tells you what you now already know: "Over 3,500 funds participate in the Mutual Fund OneSource service. Only these funds, including Schwab Affiliate Funds, are eligible for the OneSource Select List. Schwab receives remuneration from fund companies, and/or their affiliates, in the Mutual Fund OneSource service."

So, if you want to make the grade and be judged on your merits, you still have to pay to get into the contest. At least Schwab is making a reasonable attempt at showing you the best of those that would put your interests second to raising money on Schwab's supermarket. There is a way to beat the game, but you will have to keep reading until Exchange Traded Funds, or ETFs come onto the scene in Chapter 8.

No Stockbroker Is an Island

Pushing funds to meet the demand of investors who are already used to them from their 401(k) plans was just meeting market demand. Despite the problems with how funds are distributed and hidden fees that go along with them, many people benefited from the *diversification* and simplicity of mutual funds. Add to this the Individual Retirement Account (IRA), originating in 1974, and you had a fully invested public. Still, not everyone was ready to buy into mutual funds. It took an army of salespeople to change the behavior of thousands of cold-calling cowboys. I know this because I was one of those converted.

When I started in the business, pretty much everyone I knew was a stockbroker. We even called ourselves stockbrokers. Back then it wasn't a bad word. Sure, there were online brokers that could execute trades more cheaply, but people wanted to talk to a guy or gal who was their window to Wall Street. Many of us learned how to recite lines from what was then called the infamous Lehman Black Book. This was not a book issued by Lehman Brothers, nor was it a black book. Usually, it came in the form of a three-ring binder with photocopies of pitches, stories, and rebuttals that brokers had passed around Wall Street for literally decades. One of the great copies I have seen over the years included pitches all the way back to the 1960s from firms like Lehman, Bear Stearns, and the infamous Drexel Burnham Lambert. Other than Drexel, this lineup would not be ironic until after the 2008 crisis, when the first two famously went down in flames.

diversification   Reducing risk by investing in a variety of assets. However, this assumes that the basket of various assets have returns that are highly uncorrelated. If you buy two stocks versus one, it doesn't help if both stocks follow each other all day. Diversification became popular in the dot-com boom when suckers would buy a dozen tech stocks to diversify. Also common today with advisers who suggest that owning a dozen mutual funds that invest in the same stock market is diversification.

The main goal of the black book was to get people to buy. The key step in all of this was to keep it simple. If you said too much the client would get confused and not buy. Remember that we were selling stock over the phone, not face to face in the client's hometown. Boy, have things changed. First, old-fashioned straight commission stockbrokers are few and far between. Why? The SEC and Financial Industry Regulatory Authority (FINRA) had a lot to do with it. After the dot-com crash there was a push to curb the expensive and, at times, abusive commission business. On the other side the full-service stockbrokers were competing with discount brokers for revenue. While cold-calling cowboys are all but forgotten, how can the current system keep you off your dime? If the original days were about limiting information, then the 24/7 Internet world would be all about too much information (TMI).

There are a few classes of TMI to address. First, we have the institutional investors that receive research by the pound. Since the traditional research departments were forever changed after May Day, there has been an increase in the competition to provide up-to-the-minute information in order to retain some amount of profit from executing trades. This isn't a huge issue, since any reasonable pro can decide if the information is worth paying a few pennies more on a trade (with their clients' money) for an edge. The next place that Wall Street sinks their claws into is the newly minted independent adviser. Registered Investment Advisers (RIAs) are the fastest-growing segment of the adviser world and have changed the way advice is delivered to Main Street. My issue here is that a single operator can get overwhelmed by running a business, managing clients, and having time at the end of the day to filter through the avalanche of research passed along by helpful fund wholesalers. Last come the people walking on Main Street, or more likely, in front of their computers watching financial news on a constant stream that was unavailable just 10 years ago. While I have addressed the madness of institutional research, we still need to understand what caused attitudes to change over the years. It was not just the Internet, and actual people were involved.

Mutual fund wholesalers are the drug reps of the investment industry. Over the years I have discovered how to use them to my advantage, but in the early days I didn't even know what the game was. As I look back at how the last holdouts to fund investing, stockbrokers, were converted into loyalists, there was a trend of information overload that was a contributing factor.

I remember back in the 1990s, as a new guy in the business, when wholesalers started to stop by my first brokerage firm. The first guy to come into the office was selling John Hancock's Regional Bank Fund, which bought small banks that would hopefully be bought out by bigger banks. For some reason there was food on the table, which apparently he brought in—nice guy. He handed out some colorful information sheets (we call them tear sheets in the industry—on the Internet they are called factsheets). I was completely confused about why he was there. His pitch was about some mutual fund his firm sold. Was he lost? Did he not know what kind of monkey house he had been let into? We sold stock to people who bought stock. I thought the idea was interesting and the manager had a decent long-term track record betting on the consolidation of the banking industry. Nobody else cared and eyes were either glazed over or fixed on the sandwiches. Before people started to stand up and leave the room he reminded us that the fund paid a 5 percent commission. Pass the sandwiches! After getting our attention, he laid out the plan. Up until now our crew had been selling stock, the risky part of investors' portfolios, but the real money was someplace else. If we wanted our clients' safe money (did we really want this?), then the 401(k)-rollover market had to be hit. Back then self-directed 401(k)s were not common, nor are they today. A self-directed 401(k) is a 401(k) where an investor could buy individual stocks and blow up their retirement savings on their own. Most of the time you had to buy mutual funds from a select group of crap that was provided by your company's retirement-service vendor. When it was time to roll those assets over, the worker was already used to having mutual funds. So, why not take the path of least resistance and sell investors a vehicle, mutual funds, that they were already used to? We already knew it was easy to sell hot stocks to people who were looking to buy hot stocks.

It was true. Most of the money we were running was in taxable accounts and rarely did we ever see money come in from a 401(k) rollover. We were trading with play money. We provided a service otherwise known as the action that people couldn't get with their retirement accounts. In order to gather more money under our control, the wholesaler suggested we start selling mutual funds. They were marketed as less risky because they invested in lots of stocks. But, we told him, we invested in lots of stocks too! He agreed, with a puzzled stare, but continued to extol the virtues of a diversified portfolio as defined by many funds, not many stocks. To be fair, a diversified portfolio for us was 5 to 10 stocks, which is still considered fairly focused. While we didn't care or get it at the time, the bottom line was that his pitch was all about getting the safe money. Needless to say, we didn't much care for what the funds did, as they all looked the same. Most of the charts showed a comparison of that fund's performance with the S&P 500. Some of the funds showed a little better return than the S&P and some didn't, but the wholesalers would only show the funds that were doing better at the time (or the recent past) in order to entice us to follow the hot investment. My buddies at the firm were no dummies. We could see nothing special was happening in these so-called mutual funds. This was just not what we set out to do, but money talked.

What did we do? We tried it. It worked like a charm. Money started to pour in as people who had otherwise seen us as stock jocks could send us money for safe things like mutual funds. Problem was, stock mutual funds are just that—a bunch of stocks with the same risks as the individual names we were selling. It is true that having a diversified portfolio is better than a couple of hot stocks, but it was the first time I started to notice how investors see the world. On a relative basis, funds have less information day-to-day than stocks do. You don't see your mutual fund's ticker flying around on CNBC every hour. There are no earnings announcements for your mutual funds. However, clients still looked at the fund as a singular investment. It had a ticker, and the price went up and down each day. Clients would still judge it like they would a stock, but they would have less information to call you about.

As a high-producing band of young and impressionable youths, our office was soon visited by more fund wholesalers with increasingly complex stories. First it was the growth versus value stock guys. These people would explain how some stocks were high growth with big potential and other stocks were cheap and paid solid dividends. Only it was the same guys! They would come in and explain why our clients should buy not just one fund, but two different funds. The reason was simple. Two charts were displayed—this time over lox and bagels—which showed that over a 30- to 40-year time frame growth stocks did better in some years and value stocks did better in other years. Don't bother telling them everything came to the same place in the end. Don't bother asking why you would just buy the whole basket and have mediocre years all the time. Just don't bother asking them anything because they had enough information to put us to sleep. Buy both funds and you are doing your clients a favor.

There was no favor. All that was happening was the creation of more cryptic information that you could throw at clients so they felt a magical solution existed if you followed the right advice. Problem was, new magical solutions were coming in every week. A lot of the guys around me were, for the most part, confused from the start. They started asking me when we could sell this stuff and buy something else. I didn't know and was under the impression you were supposed to hold the funds for some unspecified long period of time. In fact, it never occurred to me when the appropriate situation was to sell a fund. Nobody had ever educated us on this. The wholesalers were clear: You sold another firm's fund to buy theirs. That was easy. Case closed.

Not much of this caught on until the dot-com crash killed off the old-school brokers and paved the way for fee-only advice. In simple terms, most reformed stockbrokers, now called advisers, didn't know much about picking stocks. It was just easier to buy a mutual fund and have some other pro do it for you. Because fees in a mutual fund are not a line item on a brokerage statement, clients don't really know what they are being charged. Like fast food, mutual funds allow advisers to throw together portfolios that come with tons of interesting information and fact sheets to keep clients amused and entertained. On the front line is a thundering herd of wholesalers that come to your town looking for a chance to meet with advisers.

It goes like this. A person calls my office and somehow gets past the gatekeepers. They say that they are my assigned rep for the XYZ family of funds. It just so happens they will be in my town next week. Could they come and talk to me? Some offer to buy me lunch, dinner, or whatever it takes to get into the office. Their job is to be personable. If you like them, there is a higher chance that you will buy the funds they represent. The smart wholesalers will have a fund lineup, but then try to give you the inside scoop of which funds are hot versus the mediocre managers. This is supposed to make you feel like you received a piece of inside information that will make you look like a star in your clients' eyes.

Not to be offensive, but most of these people don't know the first thing about investing. They are just salespeople. This is a problem only because advisers are many times no better educated. Each party is trying to get something. The adviser needs a story to tell their clients when they call and ask about their portfolio. Wholesalers are compensated based on the number of advisers they see and the amount of inflows they generate into the funds they're slinging. In defense of these people, they will claim that their job is to educate professionals about the products. My response? They are mostly idiots who couldn't educate a cat. You can quote me on this. Pass along my contact information. Don't get me wrong, there are some good perks. I have been flown around the country and put up in nice hotels for so-called due-diligence meetings. These meetings have some educational value, but all of it is geared to illuminate how a fund family has the answer to your questions. I get the value out of it that I need, and along the way I meet a few interesting people. For that, I will simply tell you any broken system has a silver lining.

There are some fund families I do get value from, but usually they are on the cutting edge of portfolio theory and don't get the attention they deserve. Still, most fund companies I hold in high regard continue to hire morons that don't understand the decent offerings of their company. It's sad. Most of the time I have to request to speak to the portfolio manager directly. This is actually useful, since the average adviser wouldn't know what to ask a portfolio manager if his or her life depended on it. I doesn't hurt that I am a regular on CNBC and a past character on Wall Street.

CHAPTER

Liquid Casino

When Congress started studying fixed commission rates in the 1960s and early 1970s, it was about unfair trade practices and best execution. Do we even wonder now about where our orders go after the click of the mouse? Over the past 40 years we have been setting up the largest computerized gambling hall in history. In order to create the environment where billions of shares can fly across electronic networks, we need to understand why they were developed in the first place.

Liquidity Is God

Without the ability to find the other side of the trade, there is no market. In order to understand why this is, I have a cute little story from my past. When I was a kid, I used to love to watch *The Price Is Right* at Grandma's house. One of the first things I noticed was that Bob Barker would refer to the "manufacturer's suggested retail price."

Now Grandma had severe arthritis, so at a young age I used to do her grocery shopping. Armed with a list and cash from her Social Security check, I would troll the aisles of Raley's supermarket in Modesto, California, looking to get the best prices. Problem was, the prices at the local market were always different from what I saw on TV. Barker set the reference point, and I was trying to beat it. A value investor was born! What I didn't understand at the time was *liquidity* played a big role in pricing those goods. Supply and demand was happening all around me, especially at the head of the

> **liquidity**   Liquidity is not only the willingness to buy or sell securities, but the thing that makes a market work. All periods of extreme volatility or crashes occur when there is insufficient liquidity. It rhymes with utility for a reason, for without it the lights do not go on. Put another way, people panic when there is a line in front of the supermarket and nothing on the shelves. If you don't have the other side of a trade, the price might as well be zero.

aisles, where store management sought to find the price at which people would stock up on a product.

Decades later, I now play another game called the capital markets, which differs in a few critical ways. We need to understand how the market prices securities, why you are always buying price, not the product, and how our habits are affected by recent history.

Have you ever asked someone, especially a stockbroker, why the market went down that day? Did you get the response "more sellers than buyers?" That answer underlies the fundamental misunderstanding of how the markets work. In every market session from the beginning of time, there is a buyer and a seller. Both are needed to complete the transaction. If not, trading is halted and nobody moves. This is one reason many exchanges have circuit breakers to halt trading in a particular security or the whole exchange if prices go beyond a corridor or 5 to 10 percent in a short period of time. If prices move too fast, the risk increases that liquidity will disappear right at the moment it is needed the most.

So, what changes the price? If you have more people who are willing to sell at the current market price than people who are willing to buy at a set limit, the price goes down. Think of it this way. Say you want to sell your house today for $100 (yes, you live in Detroit). If only one person walks by and offers $50, that's the price you can sell for. If two people will pay $100, the price might rise until one backs down. In each case, the transaction price is based on what the other person is willing to pay; either a limit they set, or the market price you accept. When the market declines quickly, as we saw in the Flash Crash of May 6, 2010, many orders were placed to sell at the market price. Because there were not enough orders to buy at the market price, stocks fell until the market found a price that buyers were willing to pay. That is why the market didn't go to zero that day. At some point orders came in, or limits were hit to buy shares at the specified prices. So, the next time someone tells you there were more sellers than buyers, you can tell him there were equal amount of both, but more liquidity takers on the buy side. Wait for the bewildered look.

Markets run on bids and asks. The bid is the price that one person is willing to pay for a stock. The ask is the price a person is willing to sell a stock. In between those two prices is the spread. When people jump to the exits, it takes the liquidity away from the current bids, as those bidding for the stock fill market orders. Traders call it "hitting the bid," and this will lower the price of the stock if nobody wants to offer a bid at the current price. See how it didn't matter that people were selling the stock, only that bids were getting hit so much they went lower? Put another way, if you sell your stock to the person in the room offering the highest price, the next share you want to sell will be to the person who is bidding at a lower price. If more people come into the room and want to bid at the same price, the markets are stable. The only thing that makes them change price is when the liquidity, or people offering the current bid or ask price, changes. Market orders take away liquidity because they hit the bid and ask price. We call these people who submit market orders liquidity takers because they take the current offers to buy or sell off of the market. Those that provide a bid or ask are called liquidity providers.

This is why we always buy the price, not the company. Unless we buy the entire company, take it private and sell off the assets, we must go back to the public markets to sell. Who says a stock has to trade at any price? Liquidity is simply the willingness to buy or sell securities. What has changed in the past ten years? First off, liquidity went undiscovered due to an inefficient method of routing orders. When you had a big order, it was up to your broker to call around to other firms in the hope of finding enough people willing to buy or sell. Here is how it worked. You give your money to a mutual fund. That fund is run by a money manager. He gives the broker an order to buy 100,000 shares of Acme Corporation. It doesn't matter if it is a mutual fund, registered investment adviser (RIA), or a hedge fund, the point is that when dealing with a pool of money, the trades get big. This affects your money regardless of whether you own individual stocks or pool it with a manager. The market doesn't care who you are. Now we enter the point of *price discovery*.

price discovery   The process of determining the price of an asset in the marketplace through the interactions of buyers and sellers. Also known as reality versus what you think a security is worth. You may discover that nobody wants to buy your stock unless the price is very low. Or, you may discover that in order to buy a stock you must pay a premium to get someone to sell it to you.

market maker   A dying breed. Traditionally monitored by a public exchange, the market maker keeps an inventory of stocks to buy and sell. Market makers offer to buy a stock at a price lower than the sell price. By keeping this spread between what is known as the bid and ask, a market maker can make a profit over time. However, if a stock goes in one direction the market maker will lose money. It is this obligation of the market maker by the exchange to offer a bid and ask that creates liquidity. Electronic communication networks (ECN) market makers and high-frequency traders act like traditional market makers without the obligation to stick around for the bad times. This creates a false veneer of liquidity. The NYSE is the last exchange to have dedicated market makers (DMMs).

When the broker starts to move an order that large, there may not be enough current buyers and sellers to fill it without moving the market. Sellers can move the market down and get a lower price than they want. Buyers can end up paying too much by taking all of the sellers liquidity, or "lifting the ask." The first thing that happens with a big order is to find out if anyone inside the firm has a client that wants to sell 100,000 shares of Acme. This is called crossing the order. Fast and efficient, the firm can match the buyer and seller at a mutually agreed upon price. If not, the broker has to call around, literally. He can call other brokers and ask them, then go to *market makers* to see if they are game.

After that, a floor broker is contacted to start buying on the open market. The obvious problem is too many people now know that someone needs to buy a lot of Acme stock today. Just because you know this doesn't mean you have to sell the stock. I would want to know this information, wouldn't you? With this old-style system, price discovery is really discovery of some trader's massive order. There is no competition to execute the order fast, at a good price, and quietly.

What Is a Dark Pool?

Like most things on Wall Street, the name sounds ominous and cryptic. However, a dark pool is not some place you go skinny dipping at night. It is simply a term that describes the electronic trading of shares that are not reported in a public forum like the U.S. stock exchanges—NASDAQ and NYSE—which show the volume and type of trades as they happen. Not displayed? Hidden? Secret black market of Wall Street insiders? It must be new and must be stopped, right? Wrong.

First let's define it, then provide some historical perspective, and finally find out how it affects the investor next door. A dark pool is a type of alternative trading system (ATS). Who is trading or the total size of the order is hidden or "in the dark." Many players come together and "pool" their orders. Not as mysterious as you thought.

The first electronic ATS, started in 1969, was called Instinet. It is still around today and used by professional traders. ATSs are also called ECNs. Electronic trading is not new, but trading anonymously is. In the past, when a trader needed liquidity to buy or sell a large number of shares, a broker was involved to facilitate the order. Not only did the broker know what shares were in play, but they then had to call around to different brokers, market makers, and the exchanges announcing the order. Information was leaked, and people would take advantage of that information, creating increased volatility at times. Plus, it was expensive. In 2006, however, new security laws were designed to encourage competitive pricing. Thus, our brave new world.

Since the turn of the century, dark pools have been popping up all over the place to trade big blocks of shares without announcing it to the world. Many companies saw an opportunity to use fast computers to execute orders cheaply, anonymously, and quickly. It was simply the innovation of a marketplace that hadn't seen much in the way of breaking down barriers for decades. This was no more a change than a web site that finds you the best price on an airline ticket. By trading large amounts of stock away from the public exchanges big disruptions to the market are avoided. The concern? As a retail investor, you don't know what prices those shares trade for in the dark pools. Because you still have to use the public quote systems and others can do it in the back room, it makes people concerned that they are missing out on information. It is true, but dark pools are regulated by the Securities and Exchange Commission (SEC) and keep markets stable by providing improved liquidity.

So, why should Main Street care? Fear. We fear what we don't understand. First, we fear a two-tiered system: one for Wall Street bigwigs, and one for the average investor. Dark pools provide deep liquidity to keep the markets orderly. Also, those same dark pools are now competing with the exchanges to fill your order. Remember that regulation requires brokerage firms to get the best price, and at times, dark venues can beat public exchanges.

(Continued)

Second, we fear that public prices are undermined because of dark or non-displayed orders. Prices are included in the trade data reported daily, but detailed information on volume is not known. At least now, there is less chance for information leakage because trades are executed without telling numerous people.

Third, we fear it will cost more. Do you remember what it cost to buy a thousand shares of stock in 1982? With more than 30 ATSs and serious competition to reduce costs and provide fast trading, the Main Street investor's ability to own stock is cheaper than it has ever been. For once I can say a regulation designed to reduce costs actually worked! That is even more of a mystery than dark pools.

Today high-speed processors matched with sophisticated programs called algorithms can take that order and route it to dozens of venues. High speed allows the order for Acme stock to be shopped around with greater anonymity, which leads to better price discovery since other people aren't front running your trade with the knowledge of your order and size. All of this competition has brought down the price of trading. In order to add value, brokers must now create new algorithms that allow more shares to be moved faster without moving the price. Because there are so many venues in which to trade, speed and price are pushed to the limit. Electronic market making and ATSs not only improve efficiency and cost, but lower the amount of information leaked to other players.

ATSs, which are what most people mean when they say dark pools, suffer from a public relations assault from those that think they are rigged. If we can understand the myth versus the reality, the ability for abuse will come into clear view. For full disclosure, my firm utilizes dark pools every day, but if they allow for unfair trading it won't benefit my clients or me.

I hear all the time that dark pools create a disadvantage for retail investors. How? Retail traders get their orders sent though routers that can access the liquidity of dark pools. This increases the competition from all venues, including dark pools in order to get a shot to fill retail-order flow. Second on this list of problems is the fact that dark pools don't display orders. Well, you got me there! When I move stock in size I have my broker use an algorithm to chop up my order and test it at high speed across the various venues. These "child orders" can discover if there is someone out there who wants to take the other side of my trade. This works because I am not displaying my total order or identity. How is this different from a NYSE floor broker who used to have people come up and place orders at various prices?

When I was working at my first firm, there were plenty of orders sitting on the trading desks waiting to get entered. They were not displayed to the public. Sometimes I would have to tell the trader the order was "not held" so they could work it over the day so not to disturb the price. This is no different than dark pools, only the action is faster. Price discovery is about how quickly I want that trader to fill my order. Sure, if I am cool on the position they can take all day and sit on the bid, waiting for a decent price. But if I am hot to get my position filled, that trader can be told to be aggressive. Now I have automated trading tools that can shift between passive dark pools waiting for a bite and aggressive displayed venues that suck up liquidity.

A lot of fuss has been made about how much is traded away from the traditional exchanges. In fact, most of the volume of securities is traded away from the public exchanges. However, the real question people should be asking is how much of that volume is displayed versus how much is not displayed? Exact numbers change with the day, but so far it appears that around 10 percent of the volume is not displayed. What we can take from this is that while traders are holding back their total size and price, in the end most of the shares are traded with a displayed price. In other words, in the end the volume is reported, but you can't tell what ATS executed which trade. While ATSs don't display real-time prices and size publicly, which makes them dark, they derive their pricing from the *national best bid and offer (NBBO)*. All trades have to occur inside or at the NBBO price. Don't forget that ATSs are highly regulated by the SEC.

national best bid and offer (NBBO)   A requirement by the SEC that requires brokers to execute trades at the best buy or sell price. It is also the quote that most people see when looking up a stock price. This is the best buy and sell price offered publicly. The whole point of dark pools is to get your shares traded not only between the NBBO, but also without moving the NBBO. Getting the NBBO is not the trick. Moving a lot of shares at NBBO is an art and a science. It is also the pursuit of brokers who want business from hedge funds and large institutional investors.

Why Dark Is In

In order to get some context as to why ATSs are all the rage, we need to understand high frequency trading (HFT). While the industry loves to boast to retail and institutional clients of lower trading costs and faster execution, there is no charity work being done. If prices are dropping there has to be a way Wall Street can make it up and HFTs create a new crop of customers. Do they have an effect on us?

HFT is a strategy that refers to a holding period of a few minutes to a millisecond. On top of that, they execute thousands of trades per second using algorithmic programs. These strategies have replaced the traditional market makers in providing liquidity to the market. This is where the danger exists. HFTs are just clients of brokerage firms, but as you will see, they can have the same functions without the obligation to provide liquidity. Free rides aren't just unfair; they can blow up the system. The Flash Crash was the prime example.

Location is everything and HFTs love to keep their computer gear close to the action—literally. This is called low-latency trading. Data still travels over fiber, but the speed of light can't be beat. Trading this fast only a few feet away from the exchange or the ATS's data servers can make or break a HFT strategy. Sponsored access is the next logical step. This allows the HFT to use the exchange membership of the broker. By putting the servers right next to the broker's order-management system, HFTs can gain direct access as if they were the brokers themselves. This is madness! We are talking about a member of an exchange renting out his or her Market Participant Identifier (MPID) or electronic badge so some HFT can buy with an edge. This clearly creates the two-tier system that people are suspicious of. Add to that the inability of the exchange member to monitor what is going on. The whole point of sponsored access is to get rid of the risk-management and regulatory systems the member has to comply with. There is a version of sponsored access that incorporates a third party pre-trade risk management system, meaning that before the trade goes from the HFT to the exchange, there is a second pair of eyes making sure that a thousand shares didn't get entered in as 10 million shares. However, I think the whole thing stinks because you have essentially created a two-tiered structure. This has nothing to do with adding liquidity or managing a trading strategy. Sponsored access is nothing more than paying to front run orders.

Flash trading is another version of cheating by HFTs. In normal speed-of-light trading, an investor places an order to buy a stock and the broker routes that order to the exchange. Keep in mind that this is happening in less than a second. During that second, the exchange determines if anybody has displayed an interest in selling that stock at the best-quoted price. Remember that the name of the game is executing at the best price across all of the venues, not just that particular exchange.

Only if that exchange has a person willing to sell at the best price will it be executed on that venue. If not, it is quickly routed to other exchanges or venues to find that price. This is not a suggestion; it's the law. If your place doesn't have the liquidity, you must find it someplace else.

In the case of the flash order, an exchange may sell the right for high-speed traders to see the order that the exchange can't fill. By doing this, those lucky traders pay to have the right to fill it or let it

Who Decides the Best Price?

This is what the Securities Reform Act of 1975 was all about: Creating a national market system to share securities transactions in real time. While the technology has changed from the original version, we still have a central network that consolidates trade information to create the tape. The Securities Industry Automation Corporation provides the communication systems that keep the three major tapes in the United States running. Who pays for this? Professional traders. Each month my hedge fund writes a check to several different tape services. If you want to trade, you have to pay for the infrastructure.

Part of the evolution of electronic trading is ensuring these lightning-fast trades are executed at what the SEC calls the National Best Bid and Offer. NBBO is a calculation, not an organization. Consolidated Tape Association (CTA), Consolidated Quotation System (CQS), Options Price Reporting Authority (OPRA), and Over-the-Counter (OTC) are all organizations that provide consolidated tape for stocks and options. Without them, there would be no central depository of price information. The national market system allows communication between exchanges, and allows venues like ATSs to compete for your business.

go to through the normal routing to other venues. This is rigged. You can't just pay more money to see something you are about to send to other venues and be able to change your mind and fill it. How is this useful to the other venues that are ready and willing to provide the liquidity? It short-changes competition by giving a select few the opportunity to play their hands without showing them. Longer term, it undermines the incentive for traders to show at least some interest in public markets. The exception to the regulation allowing flash orders was adopted in 1978, long before the use of high-speed trading systems. Now it is simply a loophole that needs to be closed.

Now that we understand how the mechanics work, we can understand the problems. If HFTs are going to be allowed unparalleled access to the orders coming in, they have to be accountable for the orders they send out. Monitoring trade cancelations versus what they actually execute will keep the system fair. You can't just sit around and fake out the market with orders you have no intention of filling. Indications of Interest (IOIs) are the other form of gaming that needs to be supervised. Most of the time, an IOI is used to search for natural liquidity. I do this when trolling around dark pools to see if anyone wants to play. However, I intend to trade when the other side is attracted. Part of the problem with HFTs is the use of IOIs when there is no intention of backing up that order. Why is this a problem? Speed. If you have a computer going at light speed putting out IOIs, finding the takers, then pulling back the order instantly, they can bag you and tag you. The point of IOIs is to find people that want to trade with each other without disturbing the market. False IOIs are simply a way to rig the dark pools so traders show their hands, get exposed, then the HFTs can take advantage of the situation. Not cool and not the point of dark pools. There needs to be an obligation if you flash orders or send out IOIs. What institutional investors don't like is the idea of trading with someone who is trying to take advantage of them. If your broker has superior systems and smart routers, it will take care of itself.

As shown in Figure 6.1, the tip of the iceberg is designed to hide the total size and allow the fast ECNs the ability to slice and dice orders all around the world for the best possible price without disturbing the market. The bogeyman, also known as the nefarious HFT, is out there trying to use an iceberg order to raise the price a few pennies and get out fast. This goes against the concept of keeping prices stable. Long term, the industry has incentives to keep these people out since they ruin the best-price execution. Short

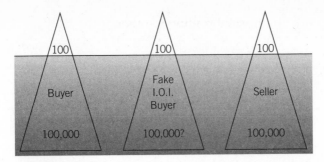

Figure 6.1   100,000? A Lie!

term, if you only care about generating commissions, HFTs will work until routers stop hitting your ECN. Thus, it is the ECN that wants to be careful of the bad HFTs, since they are the only people that can root them out.

When the Lights Go Out

It seems that after the Flash Crash we learned that HFTs provided a false sense of security. Sure, under normal circumstances HFTs are the new market makers, buying and selling all day long to bring liquidity to the market. However, when things go south, the operators just shut off the machines and the liquidity disappears. According to the SEC's report on the Flash Crash, "Still lacking sufficient demand from fundamental buyers or cross-market arbitrageurs, HFTs began to quickly buy and then resell contracts to each other—generating a 'hot-potato' volume effect as the same positions were rapidly passed back and forth. Between 2:45:13 and 2:45:27, HFTs traded over 27,000 [S&P 500 E-Mini] contracts, which accounted for about 49 percent of the total trading volume, while buying only about 200 additional contracts net."[1]

Hopefully we exposed the false liquidity of HFTs on that day, even if it took months to figure it out. In the future, HFTs will continue to gravitate toward markets that have volatility. I have mixed feelings about the HFTs. While they bring new technology in trading execution, their fair-weather nature doesn't help anyone when the lights go off. Today you have a bunch of cowboys providing us with a basic utility, not specialists and market makers obligated by exchanges to make sure the lights stay on. If liquidity is the god of markets, HFTs are the false idols.

PART

III

SURVIVING THE RIGGED GAME

CHAPTER 7

How Wall Street Sees You

Everyone has a type, but only Wall Street will take anything with a pulse. My industry spends countless hours and millions of dollars teaching people how to read people. Understanding individuals' motivations, what makes them happy or sad and fearful or trusting, will allow the practitioner to sell them things.

Unfortunately, this doesn't always help the people you are trying to serve. Once I made the break from selling things on commission to actually managing money on a discretionary basis, I had to learn how to see people beyond the Wall Street profile. While not an exhaustive study, I want to highlight the people who are most at risk of being led down the wrong path. There is no judgment about these profiles outside of how the industry can misdiagnose certain things we say. The only common theme to tie it all together is the expectation of the people. Wall Street has a way of turning your expectations into your worst enemy.

Is That Really What You Want?

A long-time client referred me to his 88-year-old father-in-law. Normally this is not the typical client profile for my firm. However, he came to me as a referral, and those get top billing, no questions asked. This doesn't mean I don't ask a lot of questions, despite my confidence that at 88 you know what you are looking for in a financial professional. My job was to figure out what the money was supposed to do for him and what type of risk he was interested in taking—or budgeting, as I call it. He quickly said, "I am an income investor." To me, that means a person that needs a high rate of income to live off of his portfolio. At this point the average stockbroker would have enough information to start putting together a list of fixed-income securities that are appropriate for a gentleman of that age. Once the box is checked, any movement is frowned upon. Why? Look at it this way, if you change a client's profile as a broker, you may have done it wrong in the first place or are simply changing it to fit the product being sold that day. You say income, you will get income.

Then I clarified his needs. He said he didn't plan on taking any money out. The goal was to grow the portfolio faster than a Certificate of Deposit (CD) and be able to get to it if he had any unanticipated needs. Usually at that age it means sudden medical bills.

Whoa! This wasn't income at all. After talking to him for a while, I realized he wanted a conservative portfolio. This does not mean straight bonds. So if growing in a lower-risk environment was his goal, why did he suggest otherwise? Because the client thought bonds were safe, he took it a step further and simply said income as opposed to growth or capital appreciation. Income in his mind was the byproduct of bonds. I don't think stocks or bonds are safe, so I asked him about his past investment experience. This would give me an idea of how he sees risk.

Here was his explanation. Back in 1982, he purchased several 20-year U.S. Treasury bonds. Why 20 years? He didn't want to take the risk of 30-year bonds! Wow, now this guy is from a very different generation when it comes to time horizon. It was a different world back then. Half of them he bought at 12.5 percent and the other

certificate of deposit (CD)   Another $3 word to describe a short-term loan to a bank. The bank needs your money for a while so they can lend it and make a spread. You're bankrolling their profits and the FDIC backs up the bet. Also known as a way to never make any real money. Unlike a short-term Treasury, a CD can't be traded 24/7 globally. Therefore, before you by a CD over a short-term Treasury, make sure you're not in a hurry to redeem it. It you want to park money, buy a Treasury. You want to trade a six-month Treasury in Shanghai? Done deal. You want to sell a CD from your local credit union in Shanghai? Good luck.

half at 13 percent. Back then that is what they were going for, just check out Figure 7.1.

Back in 1982, 10-year Treasuries sold for yields as high as 14.5 percent. From there this guy just checked out and collected the income. Beyond the luck of picking the perfect time to invest, he got the luxury of being able to mentally check out for 20 years while collecting a fat yield. Who could have known that for the next 30 years rates would slowly go down in a straight line? In fact, Treasury rates in 2008 started to go below the historic lows from 1962 of 3.95 percent and have been attempting new lows ever since. What I wanted to explain was that he got lucky and was riding a 30-year bull market in bonds and didn't even know it. He was one step ahead of me. To give him credit, he knew the risks at the time, and never expected to hold the bonds all the way to maturity. Now he was in a different place in life and didn't have time to bet on

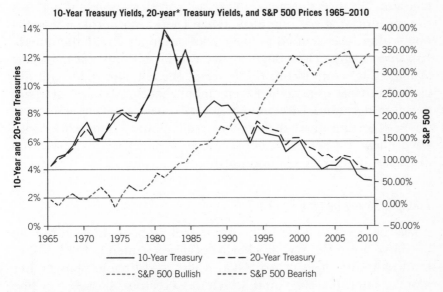

10-Year Treasury Yields, 20-year* Treasury Yields, and S&P 500 Prices 1965–2010

10-Year Treasury   — — — 20-Year Treasury

S&P 500 Bullish   S&P 500 Bearish

Figure 7.1   Did Dad Call the Top of the Bond Market?

It's easy to love bonds if you lock in a good rate. In doing so, then that enthusiasm for what turned out to be good timing may inadvertently convey to Wall Street your permanent conviction about an asset class. This is similar to someone who invested in the S&P 500 in 1999 and lost a lot of money. If you had bought the S&P 500 back in 2002, you would have made money.

* Note: The 20-Year Treasury was discontinued in 1987 and reintroduced in October 1992.

anything lasting 20 or 30 years. If only all of my clients knew themselves this well.

What could I do? Just be honest. I told him what I did was simple. The market changes speed faster than at any time in his life and at 88 he was clear on this. Then I pointed out that income, while I knew what he meant by it, wasn't really what he wanted. Wall Street wants to direct you to bonds as the place to go for security. It is easy to feel secure when the bond markets went up for 30 years, which is 50 percent longer than the epic stock bull market from 1982 to 1999. Then I suggested a conservative risk budget that would include a lot of different things like stocks, bonds, and things that didn't correlate to the first two. But we would keep adjusting the risk so it remained conservative and low. He loved the idea and in the end he told me this was what he was trying to tell me in the first place.

My point of this story is simple. You can tell a professional what you want. In turn they may simply sell you that specific thing, not the spirit of what was intended. When I was a stockbroker, if someone told me they wanted to make a lot of money, I gave them high-risk investments. How can you make a lot without risking a lot? While I was acting within the letter of the law, and made full disclosure of what I was selling (remember that stockbrokers get paid to sell things, not advice) it may not have been what the client was really expecting or what the client really wanted. This works both ways, including being too conservative or dependent on only one asset class in the case of bond portfolios.

Taking a Strong Opinion Too Far?

A favorite client who has been with me for years originally hired me for one reason: Her past stockbrokers always wanted to put her into the widow and orphan box. Okay, I also said I could manage her money better than she could, which was a reasonable assertion. She was in her 70s when I met her after an incredible 30-year run as a stock investor. While the dot-com bust had taken a bite out of her portfolio, she wanted an adviser who would let her be all equity and not try to slow her down. (She still calls me a stockbroker, which I take as a high compliment considering the goons she had to work with in the past.) Her point was clear. It was her money, her life, and she wasn't half bad at making profits. Plus, she had income from other sources including a pension. At the time, there was no money going out each month to pay her bills. I was happy to take on the business and felt comfortable that she wouldn't sue me if the market got hairy. She would always remind me about past brokers who would simply take her age and subtract a hundred to give her the "right" amount of stocks versus bonds to hold. She didn't understand, like, or want bonds in her portfolio.

As time went by, she started to have some issues with her son in Florida. While he was old enough to be my dad, the kid was having serious financial problems, and my client was nice enough to bail him out. In my humble opinion that is her choice. What is money for if you can't help your family, even if the description "deadbeat" was not used during most of my meetings with her? As months turned into years, the kid's problems never got better and my client started to dip into her stock portfolio in order to prevent financial drowning. A few years went by and conversations about how to cut off the adult child broke down and the inevitability that my client would be supporting him for the long term finally set in with me. Eventually she started asking me about lower-risk portfolios—mind you, she meant lower-risk stocks, not bonds. In the end she made an incredibly insightful choice that I would not have been able to think of on my own. She decided to hand over the daily management to me with the understanding that I would run a moderate portfolio even though that would include boring things like bonds and risk-management strategies that didn't include hot stock picking.

There was one catch. She opened an account to speculate on even crazier things like *penny stocks*. No, I am being totally serious. Now, to be fair she was only putting around 2 to 3 percent of her portfolio into this Wild West stuff, and it was more fun than Vegas, with some bets paying off like a hot craps table.

penny stock   If you want to make tens and tens of dollars, then penny stocks are for you! Penny stocks traditionally trade for less than a buck or two. Penny stocks are priced that way for a reason. Generally penny stocks are defunct firms or companies that are being promoted in a dubious way. I have a couple of clients who like penny stocks for their Las Vegas-style action. However they're not a serious investment and are more designed as pure entertainment for degenerate gamblers.

> **core**   The bulk of the portfolio that follows a strict doctrine of risk management. A core portfolio is generally a weighted average of specific markets. It's the thing that represents who you are as an investor, whether it's capital preservation or growth.

It worked. By letting her express her inner speculator, I was able to practice my fiduciary duty. Wall Street tends to want to keep you in a box or let you hang yourself. My client knew the place was rigged and wanted to have her cake and eat it too. By engaging the casino of penny stocks, she was able to experience the thrills that Wall Street is adept at providing. Keeping the *core* portfolio risk budgeted allowed her to stay out of trouble without an adviser giving her a lecture about how old ladies need to play it safe. Her last words at the critical meeting when deciding to make this change was "have fun with my money!" I assured her that running a moderate risk portfolio was a blast.

Cramer Is Driving Me Crazy

I love the opportunity to take on a client who still has years to accumulate wealth. Most of the time younger people don't have the minimum amount to hire a decent money manager—a paradox that stinks. Some individuals get lucky and either inherit money or find business success early in life. Both of those situations can lead to taking on too much risk and could blow up the windfalls they were lucky enough to come into. How you got the money doesn't always determine how you feel about stewarding it going forward.

A prospective client contacted my firm after seeing me on CNBC. After emailing my people his portfolio and filling out the necessary data-gathering forms, we scheduled a conference call. Even though the amount of assets was not the typical size to warrant speaking to me personally on the first meeting, his portfolio and age made me more interested than usual. Like tea leaves, I look at what a person has been doing in his or her account in order to guess what they might be thinking before I talk to them. The first thing I asked him was how he had been managing his money in the past. It was a typical story about having a Merrill Lynch broker that bought him mutual funds, collected a fee, and did nothing. Hey, a lazy broker can't mess much up! Now managing his account on his own he had an assortment of 20 individual stocks. At first glance they were all the usual suspects of high risk, hot stocks you hear about on TV. As it turns out, he had been spending the last few years constructing his own portfolio by watching trading shows on CNBC, reading the *Wall Street Journal*, and ultimately spending a lot of time to protect what turned out to be an inheritance from his father. Why did he want us to manage the money if he was already doing it on his own? I love to trade and consider myself blessed for the opportunity to earn a living doing what I enjoy. He was tired, stressed out, and wanted his life back. When asked if he cared about individual stocks versus low cost ETFs, he said he didn't care. I didn't expect that response. Who would put themselves through the pain of keeping a collection of high beta stocks and watching Jim Cramer each day if they didn't love it? This was not the kindred spirit I thought I was talking to.

Wall Street had sold him a bill of goods. After coming to the conclusion that paying a full service broker to buy expensive mutual funds was not the answer, he was ready for the next pitch. "Do it yourself and Wall Street will help you" was the proposition. Armed with an online brokerage account that would still charge money each time a trade was placed, along with a steady stream of noise to keep you on a media treadmill, you are ready to make Wall Street some money. Now the brokerage firm that is executing trades has less overhead and risk since the client is creating the trades and commissions without the help of a stockbroker. It is just another way for firms to make money. Let no investor be left behind.

I thought he was doing a decent job considering the amount of time you need to invest to run an all-stock portfolio. This guy was practicing a reasonable alternative to mediocre advice. However, it didn't address his issue. He wanted to steward the family assets he was given by his father for his generation and the next. The passion of the markets was not in his blood. There are no judgments for those that don't want to obsess over tickers and prices all day. Unfortunately, mass marketing suggested that taking control by using online brokerage firms was the best way to go. It wasn't like the stockbroker impressed him, so how could you do worse? Losing time with your family or career is a start. The moral of the story was for me to realize that most people don't want to sit around managing their own money, even if they can.

For the client it was a lesson that even though most salespeople in my industry are not worth the price, it doesn't mean you shouldn't look for that top 10 percent versus doing it yourself. It took me several years to find a decent certified public accounting (CPA) firm to handle my company's accounting. Why would my industry be any different?

How a So-Called Pro Fools Himself

There is a natural desire for people to either want a get-rich-quick scheme, or a play-it-safe investment. Usually it is one and the same. I want to make a lot and not lose anything—don't you? How on earth can Ponzi schemes exist if not for our ability to suspend all reason in the hope of a sure thing? I was invited to be the guest at a small conference for a broker-dealer of which the owner was an old friend. This guy used to be one of my cold callers. He dialed the phone hundreds of times a day hawking stocks. He has done well since those days, but he is polite enough to give me credit for his early education on the mean streets. Be honest—isn't it nice to have people who are successful attribute some part of it to you? Now a big-time player with a brokerage firm that has a few dozen top pro- ducers, he was inquiring about my new hedge fund. I wasn't ready to open the fund up to brokers at the time, nor was the strategy around long enough to show to anybody I didn't have an existing business relationship with. This is a nice way of saying I am careful in choosing the people I do business with.

My friend started by describing how his lineup of products included core managers. Keep in mind that my friend runs a bro- kerage firm. They don't manage money, but farm it out, which is not my cup of tea. The main group that offers the core manage- ment buys mutual funds and boasts a track record that does a little bit better in good times and slightly less bad in the down years. This is called a relative performance manager because they are look- ing to do relatively better than an index like the S&P 500. There is nothing wrong with this, and I have strategies that look to achieve the same goal. However, he was looking for some juice, which is not what I am interested in, nor what I do. I asked him what in par- ticular, from a relative performance measure, he was looking for. "That's easy," he said. "When the market is up 20 percent, I want something that goes up 40 percent. When the market goes down 15 percent, I want to be flat or up 5 percent." Wow, me too! I just had one thing that didn't make sense. Why would you bother with the so-called core manager if you had an investment opportunity like that? I will tell you why: It doesn't exist.

See, things like that are not sustainable for long periods of time. My buddy on some level knew this, which is why he has the bulk of the money in more realistic, if not mediocre, investments. His desire to find the golden goose is real to a point, but deep inside he knows that if he could find a manager like this, it would all be based on a good run of past performance. He admitted this in a roundabout way by suggesting this type of dream fund would only be a small part of his client's portfolios. This proves he didn't think something like that would be able to last for a long period of time, suggesting the strategy would eventually blow up. He was clear if he actually found this magic manager, the core mutual fund pickers would be dropped. To his credit, he is smart enough to know that if something is too good to be true, it's better to only buy a little of it so as not to blow up all of your clients' capital.

Other Distorted Images

While not a particular story about a person, the following is a guide-post of where you will be headed once you hit a profile. What investors need to do above all else is manage expectations.

Asset Protection

If you discuss asset protection with a stockbroker or insurance sales-man, you will end up with an annuity. This isn't all bad, but there are other ways to go about it that can cost less money. Plus, annui-ties are oversold and under explained. Understand that advisers or money managers are not legal professionals. While I have a broad knowledge of asset-protection strategies, it is up to my client's attor-ney to work with everyone involved to develop an appropriate plan. Nothing beats a specialist. Often, a stockbroker will try to keep other people out of the loop in order to simplify the sale of a prod-uct. If there is no collaboration on tax or legal strategies, it is your first sign that your adviser is not comfortable explaining his or her ideas to other professionals. This is not a good sign.

Buy-and-Hold Strategy

You will either get no attention or too much attention. The buy-and-hold investor is unwanted unless directed to generate some form of revenue. Usually this is in the form of convincing the investor that some stock is wrong, and must be replaced. If you want to buy and hold, please do it yourself and don't ask anyone on Wall Street for help. This includes me, and your next-door neighbor who is a stockbroker. Really, we make no money and what can you tell someone who wants you to look at their portfolio and tell them all of their initial ideas are great and not touch them? I have had some of these clients and they confuse me. I had a client who bought Citigroup all the way back when it hit the skids in 1994 for a few bucks after double-digit decline over the prior year. He bought the stock for the long term. After an 800 percent increase in value, the end of 2007 brought with it a serious decline in a few banking stocks, Citigroup being one of them. I suggested he let some loose. Why? He was sure that a short-term movement didn't mean anything. As the losses piled up and the picture looked worse, I kept suggesting that he reallocate the money, or even buy a banking index to diversify the pain. I kid you not that in March of 2009 when the market was around the bottom of the crash the client asked me what to do because he didn't "want to ride this to zero." I explained that he had already round tripped the position and lost 15 years of gains. Obviously this didn't go over well. It is simply too hard to convince someone who had an incredible run to abandon ship. To be fair, it is equally hard for a pro to accurately identify a ship that will completely sink versus a short-term decline. This is why I take my profits and move on. Some stocks will keep on going and others will fail.

Looking for a Sounding Board

By this I don't mean a client that wants to talk through his or her financial situation, but someone who wants to talk stock with a broker. This profile is a sure thing for high commissions and big paydays for a stockbroker. I see people like this all the time who want a person to give them ideas or talk through his or her own ideas. Usually they like to read about stocks and call the broker up and place trades themselves. My firm has a few clients like this, but they are on a steady path of curing themselves of it. The first thing we teach the clients is to take ownership of their own ideas and let us manage the core portfolio. Getting a professional involved in hot tips and one-off ideas diverts the attention of meeting the client's goals. Unless you have a reasonable RIA that cares about your money, you will probably be the reason a broker hits his monthly sales goal.

Desperately Seeking Guru

Yeah, I get that sometimes. If you appear on TV people get the idea that you know something that others don't. In fact, it shows that you know how to get on TV. This doesn't address your portfolio. Other typical scenarios are the elusive stockbrokers that "are always right." I come across people who tell me about those who are never wrong and have the magic touch. However, when I ask why they haven't put all their money with that magician, rarely do they have an answer. There are managers that are above average (hint, hint) and those that are the bottom of the pack. What you want to do is set your expectations high enough that a human can reach, not hold out or seek the impossible. A horde of brokers are calling people right now with stock ideas that are too good to be true, all from a source that makes all the right moves. If you can avoid the urge to find the impossible, it will not find you.

Looking for the Cheapest

You get what you pay for. This is not to say that the highest-priced adviser is better, but when looking for the lowest cost on Wall Street you will get one of two things: bait and switch, or a waste of time. I once worked at a firm that came out with some truly useless programs for investors. Charging less than the competitors, the firm wanted to provide portfolio advice to a lot of people for rock-bottom fees. Problem was, the advice was rock-bottom quality. After a quick annual conversation that was designed to get the client to confirm that their situation (also code for suitability) hadn't changed, a few trades were placed. That was it. You can do this on your own, without a rookie with two months of experience helping you. If you don't want to pay for a professional, don't pay a rookie half of the going rate. You waste everyone's time, except the firm that is looking for the lowest common denominator.

CHAPTER 8

ETFs: Fact or Fiction?

What do you call something on Wall Street that everyone has heard of, but few really understand? An exchange traded fund (ETF). At the core, they are a *basket* of securities that not only track an index, but also trade during the day like stocks. In order to understand how Wall Street rigs even the most useful tools, we have to understand how that tool works. Whatever is good will be turned on its ear to enrich the system and put you at a disadvantage.

As a professional money manager, I tend to forget that clients are not aware of every nuance of the market, or even if they care. However, sometimes a major industry-changing event happens and I find it astonishing when most people appear to be on the dark side of the moon. This is incredible when ETFs are being touted as the single most important tool for the everyday investor. Looking at industry-specific trade publications, you would think ETFs would soon overtake the world. The first ETF was born in 1989 on the Toronto exchange and at first ETFs were used mainly for trading,

basket When I was a kid, you used to be able to buy a grab bag of comic books. It was assumed that within the bag that you got a general sampling of comic books of the time. ETFs are similar. You presume you're getting a sampling of whatever the name of the ETF is until you actually delve deeper and see what's in the basket. Outside of the major, highly traded ETFs, most of the so-called baskets are cryptic, poorly performing, and expensive. Basket case is a slang term for an obsessive ETF trader.

not investing. But in 1993 the mother of all ETFs was born: The Standard and Poor's ETF which tracks the S&P 500, the most-respected stock index in the world. The ticker is SPY, but traders simply call them spiders.

So why were they invented in the first place? Simple: Stock exchanges wanted to compete for speculators who traded indexes all day. That's right, the sole purpose was to capture business from the futures exchange. Now they are quickly becoming a staple in many portfolios because they are cheap, tax-efficient, and tradable during market hours. However, just because something is an ETF doesn't mean it will have those attributes. Now they are sold to the public as a cure-all, ranging from the ultimate in long-term passive investing to high-octane leveraged bets on specific commodities like gold and oil, creating access to markets not previously open to most individual investors. Breaking down boundaries can have unintended consequences. You can expand your mind to the point of losing it.

There has been an explosion of ETFs that short the market with double or triple leverage. Listen to me now: Professional traders don't use these tools. Without boring you, let's just say we have more precise ways of accomplishing these trades. Wall Street designed them for the retail crowd, not professionals. Unsophisticated investors and their advisers are using these tools without understanding what they are. If that isn't enough of a warning, keep reading.

So, now that ETFs exist, what does Wall Street want to accomplish with them? Not since the discount commission wars has there been a race to the lowest fees. The question is, why is Wall Street so eager to sell cheaper things to the public? Remember, my industry doesn't lower fees to help you; it is designed to help Wall Street. Ultimately this is simply destructive capitalism.

Brokerage firms are finding it hard to make money as prices drop just like they did for computers over the last 30 years. Computers can do more than they did back in 1980, but is that the case with brokerage firms? Let's be honest, real talent will gravitate toward the hedge fund community because of less regulation and more freedom to be the best. Brokerage firms know this, so they have to get you in the door with something, and cheap access to ETFs is one of those tools. None of this is wrong, but giving the public the idea that ETFs' low fees are the secret to successful investing is not the whole story. Why? Because ETFs are simply baskets mirroring indexes, so you still have to provide the secret sauce. Just as corporations passed along the burden of retirement to employees with the death of pensions, Wall Street is selling ever-more-complex ETFs so you take all the risk and they get all of the assets with little responsibility. On top of that, you pay a commission every time you buy or sell an ETF. By stripping away the active management of a mutual fund, ETFs effectively throw the individual investor to the wolves if they don't have a plan. It was not much better when mediocre mutual fund managers were the only alternative, but at least people could do their homework and find decent managers. That era is fading. My industry thinks what is good for you is the cheapest, mindless, and voluminous array of baskets and niche products that you can invest in on your own. This new way mirrors consumer goods. Most people are trying to get to the cheapest price by competing with Wal-Mart, or on the other side, creating higher-end goods that appeal to quality and style. Everything else is just waiting to die.

Now that you have a primer on the landscape, let's delve into specific areas where the system is designed to work against you.

What Is an Index?

Do you ever wonder what it really means when people say the market went up or down 100 points? Let's take a step back and understand what a stock market index really is.

Back in 1896, Charles Dow created the oldest and most watched index in the world, the Dow Jones Industrial Average, or the "Dow." In 1957, another company invented the S&P 500, which is now considered the very definition of the market.

However, indexes are nothing more than a benchmark or reference point for the market. God did not hand them down on stone tablets and they were not created by the government. They are created by companies to make money. In fact, the S&P 500 is a product put together by a team of people who work at Standard & Poor's, a ratings agency that sells information to investors.

These are useful products. Professionals use them to measure their performance. But why should you care? Indexes are sold to other companies who make index mutual funds and exchange traded funds that mirror the components of that index. So before you invest in something that "tracks the market," figure out what that market it is and who's measuring it.

Selling the Sizzle

The early days were simple. If you wanted to trade the S&P 500 index during the day or short term, you simply bought SPY. Options were available for them, so if you wanted an easy way to understand a hedge against your stock holding, it was just a click away. When ETFs were relegated to index funds, nobody worried about how they really worked. The point was that they did work, were liquid, and soon became the top-traded securities on the New York Stock Exchange. I initially learned about them while working at my first brokerage firm. Guys would come up to me looking for a calculation on how to hedge a tech portfolio using the newly-minted NASDAQ 100 ETF, the Qs, named for its ticker symbol QQQ, which started trading in 1999. Back then we didn't worry about how ETFs worked or the structure because we were well aware of the basket that they were supposed to track. In 2000 all of this began to change when Barclays started to move the ETF revolution into the hands of the individual investor. None of this was wrong, but up until that time everyday people didn't own ETFs, nor understand them in general. What was about to happen was a resurgence in indexing, or passive investing. ETFs were supposed to allow long-term investors a cheap and easy way to grow their money with less expense than mutual funds and more diversification than buying a few stocks. The plan worked too well, and then the baskets kept increasing.

You see, Wall Street will lure people in with ideas of a better mousetrap, which ETFs were to a large extent. Once in the system, you will be fed more and more options until you slowly forget what your plan was in the first place. Let's look at the most basic example of how things got out of hand quickly.

We are told by those that sell ETFs that passive investing is cheaper, better performing, and tax-efficient. This only occurs if you buy and hold an index ETF forever. You are then sold the bill of goods that says that active managers are risky and unpredictable. I hear that, most of them are. There are just too many mutual funds out there trying to beat the same index. Somebody has to be in the bottom half. When looking at the steady growth of ETFs versus active mutual funds it doesn't tell you the whole picture. Just because people are using ETFs more doesn't mean they are simply holding them. This is no different than investors who keep buying and selling their mutual funds. There are three questions the ETF industry hammers over and over to pull you in. Do you believe that markets are *efficient?* Do you believe that some managers can consistently beat the benchmark? Do you believe that you can find those managers?

What a scam! Breaking down this thinking will unravel the game. First, I don't think the average investor has any real idea about what it means for a market to be efficient or not. This is a vague academic idea that has no specific frame of reference to measure it. Markets are sometimes efficient and sometimes chaotic. It depends on what market at what time. What they are really saying is that nobody can beat the market because all of the information is available to everyone all the time. Yeah, right. We all sit around watching all the news about everything endlessly? This is not how money is managed or investment decisions are made. There are millions of ways to make or lose money in any market. The question should really be do you want to invest in a benchmark that others will compare themselves to? This is now an honest question. It says you don't want to compete, you want to be in the middle and let winners and losers sit on either side.

The second question appeals to the populist anger at Wall Street. By asking people if they think some managers can consistently beat their benchmark, it suggests an unfair system you are not a part of. Clearly, some people have made money for long periods of time over and above the masses. What the question is suggesting is that anyone that is doing well will fall out of favor eventually. To some extent this is true. Warren Buffet doesn't beat the market every year. My issue is not that the question suggests there are a lot of worthless managers out there—there are—but there is no

market efficiency   A mechanism by which academics get away with presenting ridiculous financial theories based on an idea that everybody acts rationally. I was once at a McDonald's where things were fairly efficient, but never have I seen a market run like that. You order a cheeseburger, and you get a cheeseburger, just like you expect it. It suggests that information, by virtue of the Internet, reaches everybody's minds at the same time so we can collectively make the right rational decision at once. People who use this theory are using it to say we all think the same thing.

context to the benchmark they speak of. People will always think of the "market" as the Dow Jones Industrial Average or the S&P 500. Never is there any mention of absolute return strategies or pure-risk budgeting. You are led to believe that a benchmark is the only thing that matters and a passive ETF will save you.

The last question just baits people to bite or walk away. Asking if you think you can find those managers is just rude. Face it, most of the top talent has gone to the hedge fund industry, where less regulation and fatter compensation keeps star traders happy. While there are some great funds out there—some friends of mine run them—usually they are for niche sectors of the market or specialty strategies that don't fit a typical benchmark. When you buy a mutual fund you hire a person to run your money. If they are just trying to beat a benchmark buying the stocks in that benchmark, good luck.

After being confronted with some pointed questions used to promote ETFs, investors will then start to exit those expensive mutual funds. Reasonable portfolios can be designed with lower costs and transparent holdings. You see, I use ETFs all the time. They work, but you still have to manage the indexes. What they offer my clients is the ability to capture exposure to a particular index, but the secret sauce still has to come from someplace else.

Getting Down to Earth

Here is the core of what bothers me about the public's interest in ETFs. People get so convinced that ETFs are fair, cheap, and against high-priced managers that they forget Wall Street has put the decisions into their hands. Was this what you really wanted? Did you want to construct a portfolio that your retirement is based on all by yourself? Perhaps, but what I see are people that take an idea they read about in the paper and buy an ETF that fits the bill. For instance, we are in a time of rising energy prices. Why not just put some of your portfolio in the Energy Select Sector SPDR (XLE) and ride the wave? What is XLE in the first place?

The same people that brought you SPY cut up the companies that make up the S&P 500 into nine categories, or sectors. Oil, gas, and energy equipment and services are part of the energy sector of the total index. The costs are still lower than buying all of the stocks in that sector for most people, and most of the positive points about

ETFs are embodied within this basket. The problem is most people don't understand what is in it. Two of the top holdings, Exxon Mobil and Chevron, equal 30 percent of the entire ETF. So right off the bat you have most of your money in two stocks. The top 10 holdings represent more than 60 percent of XLE. This doesn't sound like broad market exposure. To be fair, I trade XLE for the ease of getting fast exposure to the largest U.S. oil companies when I think the group will go higher, but I don't have a particular preference of which stock I want to own. Hey, a lot of times I don't know or don't care which will go up more, since the group members will follow each other. This attitude has trickled down to the individual investor.

I love ETFs and the ability to trade baskets cheap and fast. If you want to invest your money, avoid the hot new sector or flipping the portfolio every time you hear a new idea. The best thing you can do is look at the longer-term correlation to the broad market, as measured by the S&P 500, to see if a competing ETF really adds value to your portfolio. A great web site called Wolframalpha.com can give you a starting point to understanding risk and reward. If you want to start beating Wall Street at its own game, at some point you will have to engage the tool it uses. Wolfram Alpha is a project designed to make all systematic knowledge immediately computable and accessible to everyone. What does that mean to you? If you want a fast and free way to do basic calculation on stocks, ETFs, or indexes, this site can help. Like Google, which wants to catalogue the entire Internet, Wolfram Alpha wants to collect all data in order to compute whatever about anything.

The Audit Part I: Sectors

Go to www.wolframalpha.com and type in the symbol XLE. Scroll down to the Performance comparisons. The default setting will compare XLE to several benchmarks, including the S&P 500. In the last column is annual volatility. This is your risk. Don't worry about how all of this is calculated or variations on measuring risk. What is important is observing that XLE is more volatile than the stock market. This makes sense if for no other reason than that it is a less-diversified basket of companies. How much more volatile is XLE versus the market? When I looked, it was about 45 percent more volatile. If you were going to invest in a focused subsector of the market which is 45 percent more volatile, wouldn't you want to get paid for it? In this case you would have, with a return of 50 percent more than the stock market. Yes, you did get 5 percent more return after adjusting for risk. Does this mean it was a good thing to have?

My second place on the Wolfram Alpha page is the correlation matrix. This long name simply means how much the return of XLE can be explained by the S&P 500. For example, if the correlation is 1, then at least statistically, the two securities move in the same way. Sure, they may not on any given day but for the most part over time they do. If the correlation is −1, they will move in opposite directions most of the time. Many bond indexes are negatively correlated to the market. The long U.S. Treasury bond usually comes in at around a −0.5 correlation to the stock market. We see this all the time: When stocks go down, bonds go up. Here we get into the depths of portfolio management that make people fall asleep and other pros get upset with our different opinions. Here is a rule of thumb: If the correlation to the stock market is more than 0.8, that thing is moving with it. This means you better get paid to take the risk, or why bother? Well, for starters, you could have a stock or sector index that doesn't move with the broad markets at all. If the return and risk are similar, but the correlation is low—you have a winner! This is what building a diversified portfolio is all about: Finding things that do well over time, but don't move with each other.

My point about XLE is not that energy is a good or bad sector to be in. It has done well over the last year compared to the market, but was also a wilder ride. Add to that the high correlation and you get a sector ETF that was essentially a leveraged bet on the S&P 500. There are a few sectors inside the S&P 500 that have less correlation. Telecom stocks tend to be defensive plays. One of the sector ETFs that tracks it, XTL, has a correlation around 0.6. This is still considered correlated, but weaker than its energy cousin.

There are still fundamental ideas that I look at when investing money. Will the government keep printing too much money? Will the Middle East cause oil disruptions? Will the U.S. housing market ever come back? Problem is, these are long-term questions that could end up with a different outcome than anyone today can understand. So keep your fundamental ideas, but don't blindly invest with them. Use the available information Wall Street uses to figure out how to construct a portfolio that has a measurable risk. Don't clutter up or make concentrated bets if the statistics don't back up what you are thinking. You can still think differently from the crowd, and I encourage it, since most market participants still work from fear and greed.

Now that you have a glimpse into how you might go about comparing the risk, reward, and correlation of sector ETF, you can apply this to anything out there.

ETNs: ETF 2.0?

In 2006, Barclays Bank issued the first exchange traded note (ETN). When I first looked at them, it was not clear why I would buy one versus an ETF. The main problem was that unlike an ETF, these notes were just that—unsecured debt. This is no different than owning one of Barclays' bonds. If the company goes broke, I am left holding the bag. There had to be some good reasons to take this added risk.

Since ETNs are not equities or index funds, they don't actually own anything, including what they are supposed to track. This makes them perfect for hard-to-own investments like thinly-traded commodities, master limited partnerships (MLPs), and exotic foreign markets. On top of that there is no *tracking error* since nothing is owned.

> **tracking error**   A gauge of how illiquid or inefficient the market is. If you're trading an ETF that has a lot of tracking error, you should think about trading another market or the actual underlying stocks inside the ETF. While it can be a sign that the manager isn't good at what he or she is doing, tracking error of more than a few percentage points is indicative of an illiquid or exotic market.

ETN issuers promise to pay you the exact return of the index minus their management fee. Some ETNs pay interest and others don't, but any change in value is treated as a capital gain or loss. Since the ETN is simply a contract between you and a bank, there is no chance of capital gains distributions like mutual funds.

It is this tax benefit that creates a choice for investors. While most of the time ETNs are designed to access exotic and expensive markets or strategies, some have an ETF cousin. Barclays iPath ETNs don't pay any interest or dividend distributions. So, if you are investing in a strategy that generates cash flow, like a stock market index that kicks off dividends, this cash flow will increase

(Continued)

the value of the ETN, but you don't pay tax until you sell it. Effectively it is sheltering current income into deferred capital gains. Even though this is a nice trick the IRS has gone along with, the exotic nature of most ETNs doesn't lend them to long-term investing. Even markets I hunt in using ETNs can change quickly. My favorite market using ETNs are MLPs, but the ETN I tend to use pays a quarterly coupon based on the cash flow paid on the MLPs in the index. That is a strange idea. You are getting paid interest based on a group of securities in an index you don't own. This is why ETNs are called structured products. They are simply an idea codified by a legal contract with a bank. Trading them on the stock exchange doesn't make them any more real.

ETNs have become popular not so much because of the tax treatment, but for the exotic markets they allow traders and investors to access. With that in mind, if you see an index that only has an ETN versus an ETF to gain exposure to, take a second look. Do you really need to be reaching for something that obscure? Chances are these products are better suited for traders and professional investors who understand the risks.

The Audit Part II: Grain Wars

Global macro trading is not just a fancy name to impress your friends; it is the search for trading profits in indexes versus individual securities. While there are infinite variations on the classic approach, the primary reason for trading macro is non-correlating assets. Yes, all assets are correlated to some extent. You expect me to believe that Treasuries don't have anything to do with the price of tea in China? However, on a day-to-day, week-to-week basis, correlations can break down, allowing the short-to-intermediate trader to take advantage of multiple markets while staying diversified most of the time. Until recently, the grain markets were strictly for those in the pits of the Chicago Board of Trade (CBOT) or traders from the Midwest. It is not just electronic trading that has opened up this market, but the continued low correlation the grain markets have to equity and debt markets. Add tradable ETNs and we are ready to rumble. Let's take a look at the two main ETNs that track grain markets, GRU and JJG. How you trade it is your adventure.

First, a clear warning for investors: Don't. Commodities by their nature are never an investment. They are meant to be traded. Commodities have no internal rate of return, pay no dividends,

futures   A futures contract is between two people: One who wants to deliver something and one who wants to get something at some time in the future. Exchanges make sure that both parties make good on their promises. Alternatively, if you want to turn $10 million into $1 million, trade futures. They are designed to match people who have legitimate business situations with people who want to speculate. Traditionally, before hedge funds and pensions got into the game, it was somebody who produces something and somebody who supplies something, meaning that the producer wanted to lock in a price, as did the supplier. They met in the middle and moved on with their lives. Now it's a casino.

and in the case of grain will eventually turn to dust in the wind. Furthermore, there is a social cost when you try to invest in commodities. Grains are necessary for life on earth. Hoarding supply to make a buck is antisocial. We are specifically talking about ETNs that track specific *futures* contracts that are rolled over several times a year.

Grain futures are either providing liquidity for the farmer looking to lock in a sales price for the crop in the future or for the baker looking to lock in the cost of supply in the future. You may also be competing with the farmer or baker for the same contracts.

While the futures trader will have little interest in ETNs, they are invaluable to investors that want easy, liquid access to cash settlement markets utilizing plain vanilla brokerage accounts. Taking out the complexities of rolling out contracts and physical delivery allows the trader to focus on pure systems trading or technical analysis with less margin for trading errors. If you are not already up to speed, ETN stands for exchange traded note. Simply stated, it is debt, issued in this case by Swedish Export Credit Corp. and Barclays Bank PLC. They don't make interest payments or dividend payments, but a few other ETNs do. Another interesting side note: Due to the debt structure, the Commodity Futures Trading Commission does not register them.

Let's take a step back and remember why these firms issue the ETNs. Both have an internal expense ratio of 0.75 percent. Yeah, it does smell like price fixing, but I will leave that up to the regulators. My concern is what the securities track, how they differ, and which is more useful for trading. You will be shocked by what I found.

GRU, composed of corn, wheat, soybeans, and soy meal, tracks the MLCX Grains Total Return Index. MLCX is reconstituted on

January 1 of each year based on global commodity production, then allowed to float for the remainder of the year. Sector weights are capped at a maximum and minimum of 60 percent and 3 percent, of which 60 percent is energy in MLCX. Just for your information, this index has only been around since 2006 and looks a lot like the S&P GSCI Grains Total Return Index. Was Merrill Lynch trying to copy the GSCI and pocket the licensing fees?

Moving on to JJG, we seem to have a different beast. JJG follows the Dow Jones-UBS Grains Sub index based on the well-known, contrarian-weighted Dow Jones-UBS Commodity Index. Unlike the GSCI, which lets the positions float and has a 60 percent max weighting, the Dow Jones-UBS Grains index has a max weighting of 33 percent. Over the last 10 years the difference between the Dow Jones and GSCI is that oil has become an overwhelming part of the GSCI Index, contributing to better 10-year numbers. Mutual fund companies love to use the GSCI for particular time periods to sell managed futures funds without fully explaining that the numbers are mostly attributed to a run in oil, not a well-diversified commodity basket like the Dow Jones Index.

You would think that we would see some tracking error between the two ETNs. In fact, we see few differences between the two. Overlay the charts and they are twins. The main difference is the daily volatility. Over the past year it is marginally higher for GRU, but increases to 3 percent versus 2 percent over a five-year period. Again, this can be attributed to the momentum versus contrarian weighting methodology between the two indexes.

In terms of trading, we get what we really want, 0.29 and 0.34 correlations to the S&P 500, respectively. Unfortunately, there is no free lunch. Volatility is higher by any measure versus the broad equity and bond markets, while return varies depending on the time period. Any mean variance software will show you a low allocation for GRU or JJG. For those who have computers, it means you take on more risk to get the diversification advantage. As a trader, I will take what I can get! The bottom line: In a day-to-day or even week-to-week system, it is a coin toss as to which ETN is better except for two important considerations. GRU is about $7.75, trading an average volume of 112,000 per day over the last three months with some slow days of only 10,000 to 15,000 shares. JJG is about $55, with an average volume of almost 200,000 and the slowest days trade around 40,000 shares. If you pay by the share, the choice is clear. JJG wins the war, based simply on price and liquidity. Is there anything else?

Well, yes there is, like a perspective on why you should be trading grain in the first place. I by no means think you should go out and use tools like Wolfram Alpha to put together a portfolio solely based on whatever low correlated ETFs you can find out there. My point of going through the grain wars was to give you a glimpse into the complex decision process that unfolds when you reach for exotic ETFs. Unless you hire a professional manager or have hours to study the market, just focus on the major indexes first. Ferraris are cool, but they often break down and will cost you a fortune. This is your money. You need not impress anyone.

The Audit Part III: Junk Is Garbage

Just because an ETF exists doesn't mean you should invest in it. To add injury to insult, some parts of the market, even well-known areas like junk bonds, can fail to translate into a successful ETF. SPDR Barclays Capital High Yield Bond ETF (JNK) may be the worst bond strategy of all time. Now that I have your attention, let's break down the major issues with junk bonds, and more specifically ETFs that trade baskets of those bonds. Don't worry, there is a place for these ugly ducklings, but they are not for those trying to get fixed income risk and return. If that doesn't keep you reading, nothing will. The junk bond market developed by Michael Milken in the 1980s is predominately a U.S. phenomenon, though they exist anywhere there is tradable debt. Simply stated, they are bonds with a poor rating. Most notably, junk bonds have higher credit risk and illiquidity, but also higher interest payments—as long as they keep paying. I want to cover the problem with junk bonds within a portfolio, the true cost of owning them, and how investors should approach the junk bond market. As a warning, most investors should simply stay away. That doesn't mean they don't have a place, but like many niche markets the application is small compared to the herd of stockbrokers touting them.

There is something to be said about junk bonds and those that invest in them. Often my firm encounters clients and potential clients that ask if we invest in junk bonds. My first reaction is to question why they are interested. Usually investors see high yields as a magic bullet providing return and no risk. After all, it's a bond, right? Some clients are savvy enough to see it as a potential play on improving credit risk, which can lead to capital appreciation if properly timed. Unfortunately, not all ugly ducklings will turn into beautiful swans. The best opportunities involve the worst of the worst junk bonds, are illiquid, and end up as the hunting ground of the best hedge fund managers in the world. Not exactly the place for Main Street investors. Plus, the real trash is not available via your online broker. From a practical level, the cost of trading, minimum size, and research to do it right is highly specialized.

Adding to the problem of incorporating junk bonds into a portfolio is the high correlation to equity markets with lower risk-adjusted returns. Over the past five years we can see a correlation to the S&P 500 of 0.63. This is not bad, and some would say if this was for an equity basket, it is better than the 0.9 correlation with the MSCI Emerging Markets Index. However, when you match that with raw annual volatility of 21 percent versus 25 percent for the S&P 500, you just don't get a big enough bang for your buck to compensate for the risk. Let me put these simple stats into English. Junk bonds via the basket that is easiest to trade (JNK) have risk similar to equity markets, marginal diversification capabilities, and performance that is at best mediocre.

If you still want to invest, which my firm does in certain situations, keep reading. It gets worse. Let's look at the easiest way to approach the junk bond market: The ETF that tracks the Barclays High Yield Very Liquid Index. Whoa, did you notice that? What is a "very liquid" index and what happened to the not-so-liquid index? There is no such thing as the S&P 500 very liquid index. Remember that many junk bonds started life as decent debt, but turned into dogs over the years. In order to have something that can be bought and sold each day, you need the most liquid of the dogs. The problem is that relative to better-quality bonds, liquid junk still trades like sludge.

Unlike stocks, bonds don't have a centralized exchange. So, each trade is done dealer-to-dealer versus public markets with transparent willingness to buy or sell. Why is this a problem? Tracking error. Remember that you can't invest in any index directly— indexes are just a mathematical calculation based on a group of securities. When you actually go and buy the stuff your results will be different. Highly liquid securities don't have an issue. For example, SPDR S&P 500 (SPY) tracks the S&P 500. How well has that ETF done tracking this index over the years? Year-to-date SPY almost exactly matches the cash index. In one year, there was a delicate tracking error from the benchmark of .21 percent. In the last three years, this error was only .02 percent and since 2006 only .05 percent. Since inception it has only been off by .01 percent. The people who put SPY together deserve some credit for that performance. Year-to-date in 2011, JNK has already diverged by .05 percent. This grows to 1.08 percent and 4 percent in the last year and last three years respectively. Since its inception in 2007, the tracking error for JNK is 4.06 percent. Now that is significant tracking error! And the tracking error is not because the people at SPDR don't have a grasp on tracking indexes. If you run the numbers from junk bonds, to investment grade corporates, to highly liquid U.S. Treasuries, you will see an almost linear decline of tracking error. Just look up the errors of JNK, LQD, BND, and SHY.

If this stuff is so bad, then why does anyone invest in the sector? Most should not, but my firm has a single example of their use. Keep in mind there are many other reasons to be long or short the group, but we find that most individual investors use them for all the wrong reasons. There are certain types of irrevocable trusts that dictate how the beneficiary gets paid. For example, you may be the beneficiary of a trust, but only get the interest and any paid-out dividends. The principle stays in the trust and goes to somebody else, usually after you are below ground. We have set up some portfolios to be higher in interest income, while accepting the risk of the broad equity markets. While this may not be the most efficient portfolio, proper risk management and low internal fees can achieve higher interest than straight stock. This is not for everybody, and each account needs careful attention. The bottom line is that there is a reason for junk bonds, but harnessing their unique qualities requires close monitoring.

The Final Audit: We Have a Winner!

So far there hasn't been much hope of finding useful ideas in ETF-land outside of the major indexes. For traders they're great, but if you invest with a longer-time horizon, sectors and commodities are not as useful as Wall Street would have you believe. While constantly looking for the secret sauce of decent long-term return and low correlations, I happened to discover a little-known part of the market. Not to fear, over the last few years several new ETFs have cropped up to capitalize on it. My only hope is that it says on the down-low for a few more years.

The initial idea came from wondering what to do with portfolios with bond exposure. Bonds have been in a bull market since

1981. After a 30-year run it could go on, but don't you think that is a bit long in the tooth? I thought inflation and bond declines would have happened by now, but with trillions of extra dollars in the system, the bull run received a shot in the arm. One of the primary reasons for including bonds in a portfolio is the diversification factor, coupled with income generation. That said, how is an investor supposed to commit large allocations of capital in fixed income ETFs with that sinking feeling that this 30-year party may be over? MLPs are neither stock nor bond, but they can be an alternative to a portfolio seeking diversification and income outside of traditional asset classes. If you were thinking of buying higher-volatility bond ETFs like HYG, JNK, or PFD, read on and find another way to capture higher risk return and diversification.

In their simplest form, MLPs are publicly traded organizations that are structured as limited partnerships (LP) rather than corporations. MLPs combine the tax benefits of an LP with the liquidity of a publicly traded security. Because the MLP passes through income, the limited partner can achieve higher current cash flow, meaning the company doesn't pay tax on income by passing that income to the investor. By U.S. tax code, in order to qualify as an MLP, the partnership must generate 90 percent of its income from the production, processing, or transportation of natural gas, oil, and coal. Considering our pathetic energy infrastructure in this country, MLPs don't look like they are going anywhere soon. With increased demand for domestic energy production, MLPs need to build, operate, and maintain pipelines and gathering facilities to move oil and coal from fields to the end user. This leads some investors to see the MLP market as a kind of energy toll road. As long as people want to get energy from one place to another, the industry should do okay.

While we never know why anything happens, I would venture a guess that it is the specialized nature of MLPs that give the group a low correlation to both bonds and stocks. From almost zero for broad bond indexes to about 0.5 with stocks, MLP correlations march to the beat of their own drum. It isn't just the type of business they are in, but the small size of the industry and complex tax structure also keep most investors away. However, nothing turns people off more than complicated accounting.

For every MLP that you own, a separate K-1 will arrive in your mailbox each year (late, I might add). For the smaller investor, this is a nightmare that is hardly worth the trouble. Remember, MLPs are a whole new beast in asset classes. While they offer attractive cash flow that competes with bonds, they also function as an equity substitute. A few of my firm's clients that work in the gas and oil industry have large positions in individual MLPs, but keep in mind that their knowledge of those companies is deep and specific to those firms. I wouldn't advise trying to dive into a small market with lots of experienced players. At this point you have a couple of options. One, you could purchase a slew of MLPs to manage risk. Then again, you could also purchase 500 stocks rather than buy SPY. Let's be honest, investors don't invest in MLPs this way because of complicated K-1s that come from the company itself. Take my word for it, it is not pleasant to call the investor relations department of a small MLP and have them correct information or reissue you another K-1 for your 1,000 shares. On top of that, what if you are actively managing position size to account for risk, changes in volatility, and general rebalancing? In short, while it's possible, you're asking for a disaster. But if you prefer this method, go right ahead. Just hide your BMW from your CPA's baseball bat. The other option you have is to seek ETNs that mimic well-regarded indexes of MLPs. Some indexes, like junk bonds, are hard to replicate. MLPs are not only small in size, but some don't trade much on a daily basis. Until this changes, the ETN format is a better way to capture the movement of the MLP market. The first one to be issued was J.P. Morgan Chase's Alerian MLP Index (AMJ). You get the diversification within the asset class you're looking for and a single 1099 come tax season.

What do you give up for convenience? Tax sheltering. You pay the tax when you get the distributions versus deferring it to a later date. If you choose to invest in an individual MLP (or multiple MLPs) rather than an ETN, cash distributions are not subject to taxes immediately. But don't think Uncle Sam won't want his share eventually. Distributions are considered reductions in the cost basis of the investment, and create a tax liability that will reveal itself at the time of sale. The only way around this that we know of so far is to never sell the MLP until the end of time, which is wishful thinking. In the end you have to pay something. The choice of when to do it is ultimately yours.

So there you have it: A new asset class that gives bond and stock ETFs a run for their money. You get exposure to MLPs without the hassle of K-1 forms. In constructing modern, sophisticated, risk-budgeted portfolios, investors have a reasonable tool that Wall Street invented to circumvent an even more esoteric draconian structure from getting in the way. Is there a catch? Of course.

The postscript to what is otherwise a feel-good tale of financial engineering for the good of portfolios is the seedy reminder that an edge costs money. Within a few years following the April 2009 inception of AMJ, a half dozen other MLP ETNs and a single ETF have come on the scene. Some weight the index differently, others just focus on gas, others focus on infrastructure over production, and some leverage the returns. Competition for my attention is what the free market is all about, but we still see price fixing in this market. You could get away with it if only two players had similar products. They could just say their expenses were similar and both wanted to make a similar amount of profit. Two places can charge the same amount. My issue is not two, but six different companies that offer MLP ETNs and ETFs all charging the same amount to run the funds: 0.85 percent. This is not cheap, and the fact that every one of them is charging the same amount only proves that when something seems like it is working, you are getting screwed on the other side. While I will keep investing in the sector as long as it is profitable, there is a bad taste in my mouth that J.P. Morgan, UBS, Credit Suisse, Morgan Stanley, Cushing, and ALPS all think they can play everyone for a fool and fix the price to trade a MLP index.

The Virus Goes Airborne

From the humble beginnings of a few major indexes, the ETF industry has been busy providing all things to all people. At first I was excited about the barriers to entry being torn down. Years ago I wanted to make a bet on Malaysia. Due to regulatory issues it was hard to own stocks in that country, but a new ETF that tracked the Malaysian market made exposure easy. From the first U.S. ETF in 1993, then a handful throughout most of the 1990s, the turn of this century saw the explosion. By the end of 2001 there were almost 100, then 600 by 2007, and today we are at well over 1,000 and counting.

What initially got the fire started was competition to replicate every index known to man. Index companies get fees to license their product, the index itself, and money-management firms to make money selling that index in ETF form. Over the past 10 years, most of the sales pitches from ETF wholesalers were focused on how their index beat some other index. (There is a herd of salespeople trying to convince you and me to buy this stuff—just turn on CNBC and the commercials are endless.) Then we played the game of strategy, with every interpretation of mixing ETFs to increase return, hedge risk, impress your friends at cocktail parties; it seemed like my mind was ready to explode just thinking about it. There was a reason for the push. Unlike the traditional index funds from the 1990s, the new group of exotic ETFs carried a higher *operating cost*. Competition has helped the market, but as you can see from the thinly traded grain markets you need a lot of players to push the price down.

In the end none of this was enough for Wall Street and the desire to get more of your money. Keep in mind they are after me too. For every new ETF that comes online, there is the opportunity for individual and institutional investors to trade more. Commodities were the next frontier. Gold was the first commodity to be traded as an ETF when Gold Bullion Securities launched an ETF on the Australian Stock Exchange that was backed by physical gold in 2002. It didn't take long for hundreds of billions of dollars to flow into every commodity you could think of. Currency was next in 2005 when Rydex Investments launched the Euro Currency Trust (FXE).

As you can see, a lot of what comes out has to do with what is popular at the time. If an ETF doesn't get enough investors and traders to buy and sell shares, it will get delisted and essentially go bust. Over the last few years, a minority of ETFs have simply closed up shop or gone belly up. With little barrier to entry, anyone with some startup capital could develop an idea and put it into ETF

operating cost Evidence that mutual funds and ETFs are not free. A mutual fund company is like a group of people who put together a pool of money and invest it. You pay their expense. What's not to love? Mutual funds cost money and there are a lot of fees in there that the average investor never looks at. Operating costs are what the mutual fund investor pays for the manager, rent, lights, and everything else needed to operate.

form. This doesn't guarantee people will want it. You can do a web search for ETFs getting ready to hit the bricks. Low trading volume and lack of assets under management signal the end. The current list includes obscure things like Taiwan small cap stocks, or a Methodist Values Fund. Really? Do we really need all this stuff?

In 2008 the SEC decided that more of everything would help foster competition and help you, the consumer. More choice is their unofficial motto. After years of allowing ETFs to follow an index, regulators decided that actively managed ETFs would be legal. This took the cake for me. Not only do we have too many ETFs charging too much to do too little, now we have to contend with a market that is being encroached upon by active managers. It is ridiculous when you sit and think about it. The whole point of an ETF is to trade a known basket. Now we have managers buying and selling securities inside of an ETF instead of using a traditional mutual fund. How do they get away with it? An actively managed ETF must disclose the positions in the fund the following day. What good is a manager that tells the world their secret sauce on a daily basis? Can't we just trade in peace?

CHAPTER 9

Gold Is Money

Unless you love hate mail, why would you want to write about the nature of gold? If you don't already have a strong opinion, know that many investors do. Most of the passion is determined by the time in history, meaning there are long stretches where people are not obsessed with the metal and it reverts to its place as shiny jewelry. During other times, like the generation we live in today, volatile markets and uncertain economic output place the precious metal front and center for a debate that has both history and incredible structural change in the way we look at it. At the core, gold is the physical manifestation of money. This is why it is called hard currency. Regular currency, or the type you have in your wallet, is the paper representation of money. In this chapter, we will take a provocative approach to what is at stake, how history has addressed gold, and how you should approach gold in your portfolio. You need to make your own decisions, as the metal will be here until the end of the world and we won't. What will you *not* get out of this chapter? Simple. You will not understand what money really is. You will see that the price of gold is always in reference to something else, including other currency. Our confidence in services, goods, or sovereign fiscal policy is expressed in its ratio to an ounce of gold. If you ever meet money, tell him I would love to have lunch. Alternatively, if you ever see the actual thing, trap it. Up until now we only have an element that is dug out of the ground or small pieces of paper that act as a proxy for the elusive real thing.

Until the 1970s, there was not significant interest in trading gold as anything close to an investment asset class. This was partially due to legal restrictions on gold ownership, and the fact that most currencies were in some way pegged to a fixed price in gold. Later we will describe the changes that caused this structural change in how we look at gold, but for now, let's understand the two main philosophical camps surrounding gold ownership in relation to gold as an investment of some type.

Many die-hard stock investors think of gold as a useless lump of coal that costs money and does nothing for you, like a bad relative who does nothing but take up space and doesn't pay rent. To put a capstone on this though, let's take a look at the polite response from billionaire Warren Buffett who once said, "You could take all the gold that's ever been mined, and it would fill a cube 67 feet in each direction. For what that's worth at current gold prices, you could buy all—not some—all of the farmland in the United States. Plus, you could buy 10 ExxonMobils, plus have $1 trillion of walking-around money. Or you could have a big cube of metal."[1] I would like to add that the 67 cubic feet of gold could easily be one cubic foot, 100, or 1,000. The amount is not important here; it is the lack of production of food, useful commodities that produce energy, and money to spend on stuff. Remember that we still need dollars to buy a gallon of milk and fill our tanks at the convenience store. We can still use gold to do this, but we must first convert the gold into the home currency, or risk getting a blank stare from the guy behind the cash register. Notice they don't call them gold registers? Well, there was a time when registers did collect gold coins in them. So, we need to understand in this chapter why this is no longer the case.

Because of the lack of production of capital, or at the very minimum the production of useful output like food or fuel, the gold haters will tell you it is a simple obsession and a long-term bubble that occasionally crushes investors like it did in 1982. Figure 9.1 shows how gold could have returned very low to negative returns if your long-term timing was wrong. How would you like to have a lump of metal that paid no cash flow and lost value for 20 years? As we move forward, just remember that the point is not the price of gold, but that it is not a productive investment. The same people that would refuse to invest in gold are still out there looking to put their capital (their stuff that represents money) to work in order to grow and outpace the devaluation of *inflation*.

So Why Does Buffett Like Silver?

In addition to his stock picks, Buffett has bought and sold some nontraditional investments (at least for Berkshire Hathaway) such as U.S. Treasuries, derivatives, and even silver. While he made little effort to tout his silver trade, his point was simple: Silver was and still is an industrial metal. It is the best conductor of electricity and is widely used in electronics manufacturing. It is also one of the more expensive conductors.

In 1997 and 1998, Buffett accumulated 130 million ounces of silver worth more than $900 million.[2] Despite his distaste for gold as an investment, in his 1997 letter to shareholders he said that he had always followed silver's fundamentals. He bought silver believing that "a higher price would be needed to establish equilibrium between supply and demand."[3] In 2006, Buffett sold the silver, but didn't include this news in the annual report and didn't say what the return was.[4]

Like oil, people need silver. The modern industrial applications of silver, along with the tiny amount in circulation compared to gold, make it a true commodity versus a hard currency. Buffett recognized that people need silver more than they need gold to keep the modern military-industrial complex running. Silver, platinum, and palladium all have critical uses in manufacturing a wide variety of products. This is the key reason some investors can get away with downplaying gold as an investment while speculating on other precious metals. By many estimates, we have decades of an industrial supply of gold circulating, while other precious metals could be in jeopardy of shortages.

inflation   I don't care whether prices are going up or down. I just want to keep my purchasing power. Inflation means you have to pay more for everything. Inflation isn't bad—it just means that things are humming. Too much inflation says you've got too much of a good thing. Inflation is like being dehydrated— treatable if found early.

The second camp is all about fear. It's true; *gold bugs* are having their day in the sun with the massive run up in prices since 1999.

But they fail to mention the longer-term track record of the metal or the overall purpose for holding the stuff. I find it unclear what their reasoning is outside of the endless chatter of fumbling central banks and parallels to pre-World War II German hyperinflation. Okay, I do get it. Some people want to see the world burn

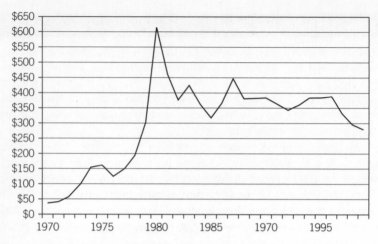

Figure 9.1   Average Price of Gold 1970–1999

gold bug   Generally a gold bug is an older man who's obsessed about the end of America and is infatuated by a shiny metal. He looks forward to Armageddon, when somehow people disregard their desire for dry food and guns for a heavy metal. A gold bug doesn't want to engage the system. He has a permanently negative view on the system, capitalism, and failed executives. He's most likely failed middle management or a retired government worker living off of a fat pension. He spends his time prognosticating about the death of the American economic system in order to feel better that all he did with his life was buy a shiny metal.

and have the only form of money that has lasted throughout the ages, mainly because you can't destroy basic elements. Nobody wants to be sitting in line at the corner store with a wheelbarrow of cash when a simple sliver of gold could pay for a loaf of bread. But is gold an investment? I am not sure the case has been made for either camp.

We will find that both sides are missing the story. Illuminating why Wall Street turns hot and cold on its opinion is what we are after. My issue today is that gold, traditionally shunned by Wall Street as worthless as an investment, is finally coming into the realm of yet another product to sell you. Perhaps it is simply targeted marketing. Is this just marketing something so Wall Street has a product to pitch to gold bugs and everyone else who wants to dabble in the craze? As contempt for the government and Wall Street continues to grow with every new fiscal bailout or debt crisis, gold will continue to have appeal to those who distrust traditional securities like stocks and bonds or those who just want to protect themselves against fiat currency. Let's go on a journey, starting with the historical use of gold.

Historical Use of Gold

There is a fundamental reason gold has been in circulation for so long. It's a store of wealth that is universal and can't easily be destroyed. It doesn't tarnish. You can melt it down to create different quantities. And if the going gets tough, you can run off with it. Before we had the globalized financial system or even a printing press, gold was the easiest way to transfer value from one person to another. For those who study ancient history, it is true that silver was the first metal to be used for money. Also, silver has had a long parallel history with gold as a means of exchanging money. Silver has a history almost as rich as gold, but to gloss over 4,000 years of history, we end up with gold winning the race in terms of value. While silver has far more important uses as an industrial metal, it is also more volatile, and historically it has been valued at a higher ratio to gold. So you have to carry around a lot more of it to transfer the same value as a smaller amount of gold. Because of this, we will focus on gold with the knowledge that silver is always there waiting in the wings to chime in. Plus, gold is prettier, doesn't tarnish, and nobody really wants to win a silver medal, right?

If you want to read a history of gold, there are dozens of books on the topic. Most are simply propaganda on why you need to buy it because of the impending doom about to rock the planet. I have a collection of these crisis-investing books published in the late 1970s sitting in my office. Not much has changed since then, except during the 20-year period after these books were written, gold declined in value. So what went wrong and why didn't gold hit the thousands of dollars an ounce that the books predicted? For the most part, crisis books on gold are based on selling you the fear that global economies will turn to rubble, markets will dry up, and you will have to use gold coins to buy food. Okay, maybe that is a cynical perspective, but the main point is that at one time paper currency was backed by gold. Even today we call it a hard currency to separate it from the paper type. That doesn't mean it has any special qualities. Rome used gold and silver for their currency like many other ancient civilizations. When things got rough, they simply debased the currency by adding less gold or silver to the coins. This is not much different from printing more paper money that is not backed by any real assets. Now you can see why the allure is so strong. These fear-based books sell the emotion of owning a pure ounce of money, unaltered by any government.

But here is where things get tricky. Gold is speculative by nature. Why? It doesn't do anything but sit and collect dust. You own it for the sole purpose of exchanging it for something else in the future. This means you purchase it in the hopes that others will accept that medium for value in the future. It reminds me of my lonely Saturday afternoon days in front of the TV. I was an only child and got acquainted with many series played in reruns from the 1950s and 1960s. One was a *Twilight Zone* episode titled "The Rip Van Winkle Caper."[5] Robbers steal a million dollars in gold bars from a train going to Fort Knox. Then they hide out in a desert cave in fancy glass coffins that will put them in deep sleep for a hundred years. Their hope is that nobody will remember the crime and walk out of the desert rich. It doesn't work out, the robbers kill each other, and the last man standing dies from exposure as he hands a bar of gold to a futuristic couple. The couple is shocked that he thought it had value. Apparently in the future they could just make gold. I asked my father about this and he told me that scientists could already make gold in labs, but that was not important. Gold came from the ground and anybody could go out and mine it. In fact, he told me that at that very moment giant earth movers were pulling gold out of the ground across the planet. This simple response from my father would stay with me forever. So, it can't be an investment any more than stashing a bunch of cash under your mattress is an investment. Nobody knows what the value will be a hundred years from now. Your main advantage is that gold will exist long after the cash has turned to dust.

If you search eBay for old stock or bond certificates, quite a long list comes up. I love the old artwork that went into the bond certificates of now-defunct railroad companies. Some people collect the worthless paper for the art or historical importance, like a certificate that references a territory before it became a state. This seems more fun than collecting stamps, since there is a story about every company. Have you noticed that most are not around anymore? The oldest company traded on the NYSE is auctioneer Sotheby's. First listed on the exchange in 1990, it was founded in 1744. Con Edison is the longest listed, since 1824. These are rare examples, as most firms don't last. The oldest corporation was the Stora Kopparberg of Sweden, which can trace its first share back to 1288. You couldn't trade it publicly until 1862, which was 62 years after the death of the Dutch East India Company. Stora aside, the average lifespan of a corporation seems to be around 40 years, which is shorter than human life expectancy. Over the last few thousand years there have been many sovereign bonds from governments that have come and gone. It is a mountain of currency that is worth less than the paper it is printed on. I currently use defunct paper currency as bookmarks, and my young daughter pulls them out of my books to play with. Along the way, most of these stock, bond, and paper currency artifacts said that gold (Figure 9.2), future earnings, assets, God, and country backed them. However, have you ever come across an ounce of defaulted gold? Even tarnished silver can be cleaned up and exchanged for dollars. What else are you going to do with that tea service you inherited from your aunt, just keep it in a box up in the attic?

It reminds me of a book, *Ship of Gold in the Deep Blue Sea* by Gary Kinder. I was researching this book while spending time in a Taos Earthship, The Dobson House. Unlike people, earthships are types of homes that don't need gold to survive; they are off the grid and made of old tires and beer bottles. I was searching for the meaning of money, but only found a warm hot spring. The book is a factual account of the 1857 sinking of the SS Central America. A passenger ship retuning from the California Gold Rush, it was carrying what was then around $2 million in gold. A few guys from Ohio decided to track it down in the 1980s. They found it, along with what had turned into a billion dollars' worth of gold. Think about it. The currency on the ship was all but worthless today, but the gold remains. This is gold's power.

Figure 9.2   **$100,000 Gold Certificate Printed by the U.S. Treasury in 1934**

The problem lies in the timing. When you buy and sell gold makes a difference. What was the price of gold in 1857? It was $18.93, which was the price of gold from 1850 until 1920 when it jumped a whopping 74 cents an ounce. You don't believe me? Check out Figure 9.3. For 70 years the price of gold stayed the same. For the next 50 years it was around $30 an ounce. Now, don't tell me that prices didn't see some upward movement during that time.

Wasn't there some inflation between 1850 and 1920? Ask anybody who was around for the American Civil War and they will tell you about food and fuel inflation. So there is a lack of living people who remember those times, but inflation spikes in 1862 at the outbreak of the Civil War were followed by significant *deflation* during Southern Reconstruction.

deflation   The fear of every central banker for the last 100 years. Deflation is the admission that your economy is not only weak but dying. The economy is contracting and things are worth less. It is akin to trying to start a cold engine in the middle of the Arctic—and it only gets worse. Any hint of deflation signals death and pestilence. Deflation is like cancer—hard to get rid of and usually doesn't end well. At best, you're a survivor.

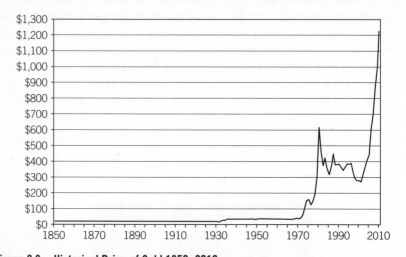

Figure 9.3   Historical Price of Gold 1850–2010
Prices for 1850 to 1994 from World Gold Council. Prices from 1995 to 2008 from Kitco.com, based on London PM fix.

However, the price of gold did not budge in either direction, maintaining a price of $18.94. Additionally, the annual average Consumer Price Index (CPI) increased by as much as 27 percent during the Civil War, showing that the price of gold had little or no connection to the cost of goods.

Likewise, by 1920 the annual average CPI was more than double the 1850 value, but gold only increased in price by $1.75 per troy ounce. That is after four consecutive years of wartime inflation, with inflation two of those years above 17 percent (Figure 9.4). If gold is supposed to protect people from inflation, why didn't it move up in value during inflation? Other factors caused instability, as paper currency was devalued and governments went on and off gold standards during times of war. Silver was still being used up until the 1900s to peg various foreign currencies. In short, just

Consumer Price Index   The way the government measures the cost of a basket of goods. Would you trust the government to tell you how much your stuff costs and what you're going through as a consumer? CPI has a fatal flaw: It does not include food or fuel. This was great in the 1990s, but makes the CPI less useful today. What's worse is that when the government creates Treasuries that track inflation, they use the CPI, not based on how much your personal purchasing power is actually declining.

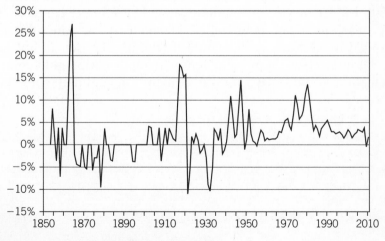

Figure 9.4   Average Annual Inflation 1850–2010

because gold and silver were being used as a standard for money, it didn't stop economic instability.

Gold Is Standardized

Many people today think the evils of economic instability started suddenly in 1971, when we generally say that the U.S. went off the gold standard. Nixon was the president who signed the act, but by that time we had already gone off of a true gold standard. That happened in the 1930s. All 1971 represents was the year our country ended the ability to directly convert the dollar to gold. How did we go from a value of gold that stayed stable for hundreds of years to a parabolic chart? Instead of going back hundreds of years, let's just start at the point when the United States decided to make gold the standard for representing paper money.

The saga began on March 14, 1900, when the Gold Standard Act went live in the United States. Everything was going well, aside from a few financial panics on Wall Street and a World War. Now that there was a standard, who needed to hold the actual metal? England was an early adopter of pulling gold from its citizens. World War I signaled the end of the British walking around with gold coins in their pockets. England simply suspended the gold standard and replaced gold coins with Treasury notes. The Bank of England started to withdraw gold from circulation. Funny thing was, they never repealed the gold standard, and enough people didn't ask for those Treasury notes to be cashed in for gold. By the 1920s, 13,575 metric tons of monetary gold was in the hands of central banks, out of approximately 15,500 metric tons.[7] The rules were changed in 1925 to a gold standard allowing the demand of gold for Sterling versus the prior system of actually having gold coins in circulation. It didn't last, and the Bank of England had to abandon

---

Gold Standard Act (1900) "An Act To define and fix the standard of value, to maintain the parity of all forms of money issued or coined by the United States, to refund the public debt, and for other purposes."[6] This was the death of silver as a competing metal. It also allowed the government to hold the keys to the dollar's value. At the time it was set at $20.67 per troy ounce. If the United States wanted to devalue its currency, it was as easy as raising the value of gold to the dollar.

all forms of gold standard in 1931 when there were simply too many people that showed up to exchange their paper currency for gold. England went off the gold standard until after World War II, when it signed up for another round of gold pegging.

My point is simple. It is easy to talk about the good old days of the gold standard, but there is nothing keeping a government from temporarily going off the standard. This is what happened in the past. We also know that when a currency is on a gold standard, it is easy to attack. The United States suffered a similar blow in 1931 along with England when too many banks converted their Federal Reserve Notes into gold. Panic was caused by the realization that the Federal Reserve was simply running out of gold. England had a good system of exchanging real gold coins for paper notes. This made it easier to go off of the standard 15 years later. Once the gold was out of citizen's pockets, central banks can devalue and control the currency with the wave of a pen.

The Gold Reserve Act of 1934 did just this. It changed the price of gold from $20.67 just 34 years earlier to $35 in one day! It takes a fiat currency months, if not years, to lower interest rates, print tons of money, and over-borrow to lose 40 percent of its value. Only a year earlier, Executive Order 6102 had been signed by the Roosevelt White House, forcing citizens to turn in their gold for $20.67 per ounce. The 1934 act, while reiterating the illegality of ownership of gold, changed the price per ounce to a level where it would stay in effect until 1968. The peg then started rising until it reached $42.22 on August 15, 1971 and we gave it up to float against other currencies.

So, what does it mean to turn over your gold? I asked a client who is no longer with us to tell me about that time. He was a young boy in 1933 and his father told him to take his gold coin down to the bank as ordered by the president. The United States used to mint gold coins as currency back then. Being a good young citizen he followed the order. After waiting in line for some time, he proudly stepped up to the teller (no, you didn't physically see the Treasurer of the United States) to turn in the one dollar gold coin. He told me it was a tiny coin and rare at the time. He was under the delusion that his gold coin would be kept safe in a deposit box with his name on it, and returned at some point in time when the President saw fit. After signing his name to a scrap of paper the teller quickly took the coin and tossed it into a large metal box filled with other such coinage. He only got a one dollar bill—fresh, clean, but not made of gold or shiny. My client told me at that moment he realized he would never see his gold coin again. Walking out of the bank he had only received in exchange a piece of paper saying the U.S. government was backing its value.

Control versus Live Free or Die

Now that citizens were not in control of the basic element that valued their money, it was easy for governments to control and regulate the currency markets. In 1944, The Bretton Woods (yes, in Bretton Woods, New Hampshire, the Live Free or Die state) agreement was signed, pegging 44 countries' currency to the dollar. Since the dollar was tied to $35 for an ounce of gold, it essentially tied these other foreign currencies to gold. This is when the International Monetary Fund (IMF) was created. The bottom line was making the power of monetary policy across half of the planet to be set by a system of rules and regulations, all coming back to the basic premise that the U.S. dollar had a specific representation to the hard asset of gold. This didn't mean every $35 had an ounce of gold sitting in a vault. We have a fractional banking system that allows a dollar deposited in banks to be lent out several times, since there was not enough gold in the world to match all of the dollars created. It was a system based on the trust of the United States of America. You see, when another country got into trouble, they would have to devalue their currency against the dollar. If foreign governments doubted the United States' ability to maintain the gold standard, they would express this by asking for the gold it was backed by. Called the gold window, it's like a foreign country like Switzerland pulling up to the window and asking to cash in dollars for an equivalent amount of gold. Sounds like a good system. In fact, if signers of The Bretton Woods Agreement were confident in the United States, they would not need to use the gold window at all.

Well, the United States has never been good at keeping a balanced budget, even though we were the economic superpower at the time. The 1960s had some great economic times for the stock market, but the gold window was starting to get some cracks in it. There were attempts to defend the $35 price by putting a London Gold Pool together between several nations. It didn't work as planned, as the economic instability that the gold standard was trying to avoid began to take over. In 1967 the British had a run on their gold holdings, forcing them to devalue against the dollar. Essentially, investors said they would rather have gold than British pounds. This is why that gold window existed, right? The French government started to turn in their dollars at the gold window to build up their reserves in 1967. By 1968, private gold markets outside the United States opened up and the price was of course higher than the official dollar price. By 1970, inflation, the Vietnam War, and government spending in general caused other governments to lose faith in the United States' ability to keep spending in line. In the summer of 1971 things simply got out of hand, the dollar started to devalue against European currencies, and we were forced to close the gold window. This forever removed the dollar from any type of gold peg, no matter the price of the peg. Chaos ensued, and the price of gold steadily increased to a whopping $154 average price by the end of 1974. On New Year's Eve, 1974, President Ford lifted the 40-year ban on gold ownership by U.S. citizens, but it made little difference.

Fast forward to January 1, 1980 when gold reached a high of $850 an ounce on irrational exuberance, inflation, and a sick U.S. economy. Iran's Shah had just been thrown out along with the government, the Soviets had invaded Afghanistan, and Jimmy Carter was still President. My chief operating officer was in Iran at the time and it was not a pretty picture. One of my clients worked for the United Nations and had to climb over cars to reach the airport— no need to check any baggage. Keep in mind that just a few years before OPEC had turned off the pump, and while I was growing in my mother's womb, she was waiting in line to fill up her Pontiac Firebird. Clearly I learned at an early age that it is no fun to have a hot car with no gas; I would have freaked out and bought some gold myself. While there were legitimate concerns about rampant inflation and a no-growth stock market, speculation was the ultimate cause of the high watermark on gold prices that would take almost 30 years to recapture. In the end, the price went up because people were willing to exchange more and more dollars backed only by faith in the United States for a metal backed by a thousand years of obsession.

Who would have known that this was the perfect time to sell gold, buy dollars, and invest in the stock market? You could have also purchased U.S. Treasury bonds paying 12 percent with that gold and made out like a bandit. Sometimes you have to buy at the sound of cannons and sell at the sound of trumpets. In this case, what could get worse? Not being on a gold standard didn't mean currency would have no value, because everyone needs currency to buy things. The long-term decline in gold was due in part to the expanding economy during the 1980s and 1990s that made owning stocks and bonds more attractive than a metal that did nothing. It still came from faith and an expanding economy.

Brave New Non-Pegged World

My point in telling you all of this is to show you how to sell your gold. Remember that gold is speculative in nature and is simply an insurance policy for the big one—not the end of the world, but hyperinflation! It's the ultimate insurance policy against a home currency (the one you buy food with) from melting down. This is precisely why über-investors like Buffett say nasty things about it. That crowd will make gold ownership out to be an irrational decision when compared to a company that has an internal rate of return. Gold has no value in creating cash flow, dividends, or

My Gold Bear

My first experience with gold came full circle by the time I was a teenager. For graduating from sixth grade, as if it was a choice, my father gave me a gold coin. It was a beautiful one-ounce Chinese Panda Bear. They had just started minting them back in 1982. At the time it was worth around $600 and that was all the money in the world to me at the time. Not much happened other than the drop in value each year that sidetracked my interest in metals for the 1980s bull market. My small collection of precious metal coins was collecting dust. When it came time for me to earn some money outside of investment activities, those coins came in handy. At the time I wanted to buy an expensive video camera. The goal was to create videos of homes for real estate brokers in my hometown. That Panda Bear fetched about $475 and was enough along with my birthday money to get in the game. When I look back, the gold held its value relative as to what it could buy. A video camera in the early 1980s was thousands of dollars compared to what I could buy at the end of the decade. More than that, exchanging the mint-condition coin gave me a tool to earn money. Outside of that my gold coin was useless sitting in my secret hiding place.

interest income. It has little value as an industrial metal, with only 10 percent used for making things. The other 90 percent is split between jewelry and hard currency. It is a paid-up policy for a hyperinflation event. The only thing that has no counterparty risk is—do you really trust the government to make good on their debt if things get crazy? Just ask anybody who lived in South America during the 1980s. Gold doesn't need the other side of the trade to make good; it is Mother Nature herself, an element on the periodic table.

Therefore, it is not an investment, but a thing to sell in the future. If you wait long enough, an event will happen where you or your heirs will want to cash in your gold chips. We wouldn't need this insurance if markets could be rational all of the time. Government policies don't always help. So, only when the political tides change can we expect a change in policy. This is what happened in the United Kingdom and the United States at the beginning of the 1980s when it seemed as though it couldn't get worse. Just remember that in the early 1930s it was bad and didn't get better for more than a decade.

Gold is money, not a bubble. But, if too many people want a currency, hard or fiat, a bubble can occur. It is the market that takes a commodity and turns the price paid into a bubble. Because every bubble can be invested in, Wall Street has convinced the public that it is an investment to hold onto. I have some, and so should you, but know when to sell. Let Greece collapse, let the Chinese make us pay high interest rates for our Treasury bonds, let the Middle East have a complete breakdown. It doesn't matter what happens in the future. When things get to the point of no return, sell. Once we all decide enough is enough, the new dawn of hope will emerge and gold will once again take a back seat. Don't believe me? Take a look at the top things that were happening when gold hit a low of $251.70 an ounce on August 25, 1999. The stock market was hot as rocks, unemployment was at historic lows, and interest rates were reasonable. Political stability and peace were in place along with a new global currency—the euro—that would surely make gold obsolete.

Now we are back to the other side, but it is unclear if this bubble will keep going for a while. Have we had enough pain to take unpopular actions? I don't think so. The Middle East is not totally messed up. Greece isn't reforming fast enough. China is still buying up our debt. The euro is becoming harder and harder to analyze with the disparity between the financially sound and weak countries inside the European Union. At least this has secured a lot more time for me to talk about it on CNBC! Mining companies are no longer hedging their production on gold, suggesting they think the price goes up from here. These are the same companies who hedged for lower prices in 1999. Will gold mining companies' hedging strategies turn out to be a long-term indicator of tops and bottoms? The list is building, but real pain has yet to emerge. Remember that when we all have to take a bitter pill, no matter what the form, that will be the time to cash in your chips. Fortunately, there will be gold bugs ready to take it off your hands.

CHAPTER 10

Options: *Really?*

Every time the stock market crashes (it happens every few years, so get used to it), people come out of the woodwork to ask me about options, while giving me their personal opinions on them. Some will simply say they are risky. Others will say they are an easy way to make money. The truth lies somewhere in the middle. If you want to arm yourself with a power tool, options are the way to go. However, if you don't know how to harness their power you will get blown out of the water.

Do You Want Them?

I want to share a little history about the option markets so you can understand why options exist, what they can do, and why they are difficult to use.

Options have been around for thousands of years, but they weren't traded for equities until about 300 years ago. Back then they didn't have exchanges for options. It wasn't until April 26, 1973, that the Chicago Board of Options Exchange (CBOE) started trading contracts on 16 stocks.

Two years later, they computerized the exchange, and the markets have never looked back; except for 1977, when the Securities and Exchange Commission (SEC) halted option expansion, pending a review of the growing *derivative* markets. Sounds like today, right? Despite the efforts of the SEC, once you give the market a toy, don't expect to get it back, ever.

derivatives   A general phrase for a contract that's based on the price of something else. You can make them as complex as you want. Everybody makes much ado about the word. Quite frankly, when I was younger, we just called them options. Calling something a derivative seems more like a need to vilify it. Because derivatives sound more evil than options, the term is used more often in the media.

expiration   Generally every month options expire and new ones are created. Expiration is really about a particular day when markets have to deal with a bunch of derivative traders getting their act together in order to settle their obscure contracts. This can cause unusual anomalies in daily trading on those particular days. "Triple Witching" is when stock options, stock index futures, and stock index options all settle on the same day. When this happens, there are too many people messing around on the same day, all with legitimate business to conduct. A slew of derivatives traders are all trying to organize a multitude of contracts.

The CBOE started the exchange to allow institutional investors the ability to hedge their bets. Do you own a stock and want to buy insurance against it going down? Do you want to buy a stock today, but the money needed to pay for it is locked up in a Treasury bond for another month? Options, for a fraction of the cost of the stocks they represent, give investors an answer to these dilemmas. The important thing to remember is that options have an *expiration* date, so you need to understand your end game before you invest.

Forget about what they are called (puts and calls) or the funny names of the strategies (iron condors and straddles), and focus on what options can do for you.

First, decide whether you want to build your strategy yourself or use a pro to help you. I find that Wall Street is very focused on getting people excited about options and their trading capabilities, but in the end wants the end user to make up his or her own mind. Why? Legally, advisers can get into a lot of trouble because of the risky nature of options. Also, most advisers would not know how to construct an options strategy to save their lives. If the industry can simply educate you, but avoid giving advice, you lose all your money and have nobody to blame but yourself. This is a poor way to do business, but look at it from my point of view: If people don't enter a new game and lose their money, how am I supposed to collect it for my clients? I didn't say this was a nice place to make money. As you can guess, the number of strategies is limited only by your imagination. However, in my opinion the best ideas are simple. Our firm does some options strategies, but they are plain vanilla compared to some of the stuff you can be sold. The more complicated, the less you can really understand. If the so-called pro can't explain it to you, it means two things: First, the pro may not know what he or she is doing (most likely). Second, it could mean that you don't have the ability to understand the strategy. If the latter is the case, don't worry, but don't do it.

Do you still think options are risky? Do you think auto insurance is risky? If you can pay a little and protect your financial liability, it's a good deal, right? But what if you walked over to your neighbor and offered to insure his BMW for $500 a year? You'd better hope he never drives the car.

Which side of the transaction you are on determines the level of risk. Options can hedge and control risk—the original purpose for them—or they can be used for speculation and gambling. Fortunately, some investors want the riskier side of the transaction. That's what creates the market.

If you want to gamble, I suggest a casino; many are less than an hour away and come with a free buffet. But when it comes to your money, don't use the excuse that you don't understand to prevent you from taking advantage of very basic, ancient techniques to protect your capital. Remember, options can be a tool to get you where you want to go. Just make sure you have a map, a compass, and a clue to your next destination.

Practical Strategies

I have very little interest in showing people how to lose their money. On the other hand, if people are going to do something stupid, why not limit the madness? We need to describe the delusion and then offer a strategy to express it.

"I Got a Tip"

Okay, there are no real tips, and if you get an actual piece of inside information you could land in jail. But, if you have a hunch, tip,

---

Wanted: Donors

How is the average investor presented with options strategies? First, they're usually not told that's what it is. Why does Wall Street like options? They're an easy sell. Every time you see a newsletter or web site touting outrageous riches overnight, it's options. Because options can be put together in a way to create virtually any type of scenario or strategy, you can sell any idea using them. For instance, have you ever seen some guru on late night TV talking about his "strategy that works in up, down, or sideways markets," or "How would you like limited downside and unlimited upside?" They're talking about options. Another big appeal is the small amount of capital needed to buy option contracts, along with the significant leverage that options can provide. Brokerage firms also make more money from option transactions as opposed to stock orders. It's a profitable business. Plus people who like to trade options are most likely traders, or, at worst, degenerate gamblers.

If you look at it another way, what if the sales pitch was "How would you like to lose your entire investment in less than a day?" Very few stocks can offer that promise. Or perhaps "Would you like to pay more in fees and be on the hook for more than you initially invested?" Try options. My personal favorite is for the novice investor to try options. Sophisticated hardcore traders need novice investors to donate money.

What makes option trading hard is twofold. First, you have to be right about time. All options expire. So you can be right about your idea but lose all of your money, because it doesn't happen in the specified time period. Second is option pricing. Options are priced using complex models that sophisticated traders are generally on top of, but the average hobbyist is at a significant disadvantage. Simply stated, they're complicated. This is why most investors stay away from them. Not because they're bad, but because they have a level of complexity that takes years to master. I personally know many successful traders who have made millions trading stocks and are smarter than I am, who do not trade options because they find them too complicated to deal with. If you're the type of person who likes to play chess or solve complex puzzles, options may be a good outlet to funnel your energy.

---

or otherwise ridiculous idea that nobody will talk you out of (no, I don't have the time and don't care) then call it what it is and put your money on the line.

If the object is to take advantage of a big move quickly, then use the tool designed for that. A call option is a cheap way to throw money away. Why? Because you can only lose what you spend on the option. In a nutshell, you buy a contract that will increase in value if the stock goes up. The catch is time. An option has a lifespan, and if the stock doesn't move in time, you lose your money. Hey, if you are so sure of yourself, how can you lose? Obviously you can, but there is no point to applying traditional rational investing techniques to speculation. You can do the same thing in reverse, buying a put option to bet a stock will go down in a given period of time.

The first option I ever bought was in 1998, betting that the price of gold would go up. Don't ask me where I got the tip—did it matter? Back then we didn't have ETFs that tracked gold, but there were options on futures traded on the CBOE. Needless to say, I lost all of my money. Sure, the price of gold would later go up five times over the next 12 years. But at the time gold kept going down, and continued to for a year after my options expired, worthless.

My main piece of advice is try to avoid this type of speculation, but the strategy is perfect for those times when there is no way to avoid stupid. Plus, it could work out, which would be worse because then you think you actually have a plan. Every once in a while I will buy some options on an index, a stock, or a commodity. Usually I win some and lose some, but over time I doubt I have made much. What I can tell you is that for me, it is more fun than playing blackjack, but doesn't come with a free buffet. Just do yourself a favor and keep the trade to yourself, if you make money you can tell them later and if you lose they won't hate you for the tip.

Steps:

1. Decide how much time you need for your crazy idea to work, or at least how long before you are willing to move on if it doesn't happen. Typically you don't want to go out longer than three months, but it can be as short as a few weeks. My advice is to give yourself a bit more time than you think. Not that this will help you much.

2. What do you think will happen? You need to have some idea about how much a stock will move up (or down). This will play a role in calculating your bet in the next step. It has to be at least a 10 percent move or you will never pay for the price of the option.

3. Pick a strike price and figure out if you can actually make some money. If you have $10 stocks and the price of an option is $1, you have to think the stock will at least go to $12 in order to double your money. There are some more

factors to consider, but you get the picture. Confused? Don't be, there are great online tools, especially from the Options Industry Council (www.optionseducation.org). Their job is to keep the industry reasonably reputable.

4. Put your money down and let the market do the work.

"I Want to Protect My Profits, but I Don't Know Where the Sell Button Is Located"

Okay, the biggest problem that investors, speculators, and even professional hedge fund runners have in common is when to sell. Add to that the uncertainty of when the market is going to take a dive, and you understand how the paralysis takes hold. What if you have a stock position that has been working for a while, and for whatever reason you don't want to take money off of the table. Do *not* try to rationalize the taxes, or that you inherited it from your dad, or maybe you watched something on the news and it said the world will end soon. Reasons don't matter; the point is that you want to protect yourself. Lucky for you, Wall Street has a market for that.

We call it a protective put. It's just a short-term insurance contract that is purchased to protect your existing stock position in the event it goes down during the specified time period. The catch is that it costs money! Also, you have to cash in the policy yourself, or wait until it expires. Nobody said it was easy, but if you don't want to part with your stock, this is an easy way to hedge your bet.

My main piece of advice is not to get carried away with this. It is best used for a concentrated position, or a stock that is more than 20 percent of your portfolio. The best question to ask is why you don't want to sell the stock in the first place. Nobody ever went broke taking a profit. Try this strategy only when you have a significant reason to expect the stock to go down in a meaningful way. At our firm, if we think the market or stock will go down, we just sell and go into cash. The cheapest and lowest-risk way to short something is to simply go to cash. No risk, no return. Keep that in mind when thinking about buying a protective put. You can never escape from risk, but you can pay to neutralize it for a short period of time.

"I Am Sitting on a Ton of Stock That I Would Like to Sell, but I Hate Tax"

Many of my clients became wealthy by holding stocks for long periods of time. Of course, you have to have the right stock and most of my clients will admit it was just hard work and lots of luck. The reason they held the big position for years is because it survived while the other stocks were sold or made their way out of the client's portfolio. After a point, some clients don't have the emotional attachment to the stock and want to diversify the holding. In other cases, they don't think the stock has the magic it did in the past.

The challenge to a client's portfolio in exiting out of a position of great size is generally twofold. First, it's emotional. The sooner people can stop making excuses, the faster they can get to the money-making part. Second, there's low *cost basis*. We have the lowest capital gains tax in decades, but tax is tax and nobody likes to pay.

One potential solution is selling call options on the position. This is a classic strategy that I cut my teeth on during my early days on Wall Street. Back then I specialized in officers in publicly traded companies. When these executives wanted out, they didn't know when to sell, and the tax bill was a lot bigger back then.

Here is the concept: Some people out there want to buy a call option to bet a stock is going up. For that they pay a *premium*.

Remember that options have a price tag on them if you are buying them. In a covered call strategy, you sell the call option, or sell short the contract. So, you are now on the other end of this transaction. Don't

cost basis Investors will do funny things, primarily if they sell $100 worth of stock, and they assume they have to pay tax on the $100. If they bought the stock 50 years ago, the cost basis could be almost zero. This cognitive mistake causes a lot people to hold onto stocks for too long, only to find their cost basis is negative because they failed to take their profits for fear of paying tax that would have shown that they won. Now losers, they boast how little tax they pay, forgetting to add up how little profit they made.

premium Options have two parts in their pricing: the intrinsic value and the premium. Premium is how much you pay to get the right to enter into a contract with a counterparty. If you're a buyer, you pay a premium to risk no more than what you paid to tell somebody else at some other time to do something. If you're a seller of an option you accept money in return for doing something for somebody later. Investors need to choose whether they want to obligate themselves or somebody else.

worry, you don't have unlimited loss because you own the stock the option is based on. You are essentially saying to the buyer that you will give him your stock at a specified price (the strike price) at a specified time (option expiration). For this you get money today! If your stock never reaches the strike price, you keep the money when the option expires. On the other hand, if the price is higher than the strike, your shares are magically taken from your account. What do you get for the stock? You get paid the strike price, not what it is going for on the open market, plus you got to keep the premium.

Why not just sell the stock? You can, but this way you can take in some income over time and slowly get out of the position. Of course, you could end up seeing the stock go down during this period of time, and if the price of the stock goes down more than what you got by selling the call, you'd think you would feel stupid. But you won't! If you have a plan and stick to it there will be no regrets. If you want to try out a covered call strategy, do your homework or hire a pro with experience with option strategies.

"Options Are Great! Why Doesn't Everyone Use Them? Put All of My Money Behind Them!"

Stop right there. The fastest way to lose all your money is options speculation. I strongly urge everyone out there to understand that Wall Street wants to get you hot and bothered by all of the possibilities and not think about why you are using them. It takes years of trading options to figure out what works and what doesn't. Every situation needs careful analysis. Unfortunately, by the time you figure this out your portfolio could be pummeled.

Before getting into an options strategy, understand why you are doing it. Also realize that when you educate yourself on the topic, real world pricing is never mentioned. From a beginner's point of view, it seems easy as long as you can do some basic math. However, option traders are the most vicious players in the business. I know because I am one of them. Don't think it is a get rich quick scheme and don't quit your job after a wining trade. These are great tools to limit your risk on stupid ideas (long calls or puts), protect a stock position (protective puts), or ease out of a big position with some income to pay the taxes (covered calls). Anything else is going into the realm of professional options strategies. If that is what you want, you are on your own.

CHAPTER

11

Dividends: A Conundrum!

Wall Street needs your money more than any other institution on the planet short of the U.S. government. So how can they get everyone's attention at the same time? If you want to trade stocks, you are the top client the industry is looking for, since you create commissions all by yourself. Buying mutual funds comes in second with hidden fees. On the other hand, if you are just looking for a few good stocks to hang onto, the margins are thin. Wall Street doesn't care and would rather have all of the business. You can't just fool some of the people some of the time, you have to fool everyone all of the time. By picking and choosing the right alchemy of marketing and facts, you can create a group of believers. Cults work, and the power of belief is the most powerful weapon next to fear and greed.

> **dividends** Portion of profit paid by a corporation to the shareholders. Also, the only way you get paid if you sit and hold a common stock for a long period of time. The search for high dividends is the primary mechanism for suckers getting lured into buying shares of companies that are going bankrupt. You're not in control of them. Management decides how much they are. It's like an allowance. You have to go beg daddy for your share. If the company is really that good as an investment, the company should really be reinvesting the money, not paying a dividend. Paying you a dividend is an admission that management can't figure out what to do with the money.

The Pitch

Dividends have been used on Wall Street to create a cult environ-ment that still exists to this day. It wasn't always like that, and things have changed over the years. We need to understand how dividends became the focal point for stock investors and ultimately whether they're the right focus to have. But if dividends are not the ultimate answer to investing, then what is?

The individual obsession with dividends started back in the 1920s. This was the decade that brought in hundreds of thousands of smaller individual investors. These people wanted to buy stock, and Wall Street was able to learn how the crowd responded en masse. It was during this decade and the depression that followed that companies formed strong ideas about how to manage their divi-dend policies in order to keep investors happy. By changing the con-versation about what made a company good, Wall Street was able to rig the system by creating a change in perception. This was a new era that redefined how to sell stock to investors. No longer was the market exclusive to the very wealthy and to speculators. Main Street was entering the market, and they needed a sales pitch that was dif-ferent than had been used before. Dividends would be the key point that people were looking for. Remember that back in those days, stocks were expensive to buy and sell. High commissions would be the norm until 1975 when deregulation started a 20-year competi-tion for the cheapest prices to trade stocks, ultimately leading to the rampant overtrading we see today. When investors bought stocks in the 1920s, they were attempting to buy a piece of the American dream and the riches that came with it.

Different than bonds that are designed to pay interest, common stocks don't have to pay anything. Every year the management of a publicly traded company votes on paying a dividend to the common stock shareholders. Nothing is set in stone and no dividend has ever been safe. It amazes me when people ask me, "Is the dividend safe?" If you need to get a group of executives in a room to vote about something every time it happens, it's not safe. Sure, there are com-panies that have been paying dividends for decades, but we also see every few years a major corporation that either cuts its dividend or goes broke because they paid too much money out for too long. Just look at Citigroup and General Motors in 2008. We need to take a step back and understand the overall concept of dividends. I am

Monopoly University

If you can get your kids to play the classic game Monopoly, financial education is a breeze. When I asked my father how $50 popped out of the sky into my coffer just because of a dividend, he explained the concept in a way that Wall Street would like to keep quiet. Let's go back to that Saturday afternoon. And yes, my father was this straightforward with a six year old. I didn't get this way all by myself.

"Lee, let me explain what that money is before you take grab it from the bank. This money you got came from earnings that a company decided to pay out to the owners, or the shareholders, and not keep it for themselves."

"I would like to keep all of the money for myself."

"I know, that is how management thinks. They're the people who run the company. If a company makes a dollar over the course of a year, they have to decide how much to keep for next year and what they don't need."

"Why wouldn't they just keep all of it?"

"Because it is not their money, the profits belong to the shareholders. Management has to explain what they need the money for and shareholders vote for what is in their best interests. Management may say they made a dollar, but 50 cents is needed to *reinvest* next year on a new plant or project that will make more money for the shareholders in the future. If that is the case, there is still 50 cents that is not being used, so that money is paid out to the shareholders as a dividend."

reinvestment   After a company has failed to figure out how to invest profits, they pass them along to you in hopes that you will buy more of their stock. While dividend reinvestment has built wealth, it's important to understand what the concept is. If a company says "We don't know what to do with the profits other than give them to you," maybe you should invest them somewhere else.

"What if they need all of it?"

"Many CEOs say they need all of it because they are liars that want the money closer to themselves than to shareholders. You can't get paid excessive amounts of money unless the cash is sitting next to you. I don't like to buy companies that don't pay dividends because they either don't make enough money to pay dividends, or the CEOs are arrogant and think they can invest every dime of my money and grow it to the sky."

"I don't understand." (I am six years old!)

(Continued)

"There are companies that make everyday things like Coke. Each year they make some money, then reinvest some of it to grow, and some of it gets paid to me. Coke knows they can only grow so fast, and their profits each year are more than what they need next year to sell more Coke. These computer companies are different. Most of them don't make much money, and when they do the people running the company want to take every dime, including borrowing more money, to build more things. If it works out, the stock should to go up, but it may or may not depending how people feel about the company. That is why we have a stock market, so we can agree on a price for each share. This is how I make my money. If the new investments are a dud, then I have a stock that is worth nothing, and no dividends to show for it. I got screwed!"

"Can I vote on dividends?"

"Yes, but you have to buy shares in the company first. The problem is, if you don't own enough of the business or if enough people don't vote with you, you are screwed. Management will do what they want and you have little control over it. The key is to see if the person running the company owns a lot of shares. They tend to do a better job when their money is on the line."

"This is cool, I think I want more dividends and more money."

"You first need to learn how to research the companies to figure out which ones manage profits well. That is why I read the annual reports of those companies. Once you have to get involved in telling a company how to pay out profits, you are playing a different game of taking it over, not just buying the stock. You don't have that kind of money, and I don't either, so why fool around with it? If the company can't handle their business right, they can pay a dividend, not manage the company right, and then the shares are worthless. It is harder than it looks, and just because something pays a dividend doesn't mean it is a good company. It's my turn to roll the dice. Get me another drink."

The last lines my father told me were the most important. Dividends as a concept are easy to understand. You get the excess profit as a shareholder. This only makes you money long term if the company can manage the business successfully, and dividend policy is a critical piece of the process.

not talking about what they are, but how an investor should look at them. As it stands now, most people have been trained by Wall Street to ask the wrong questions. We want to understand why.

The Early Days

Just to spoil everyone's day, everything you really need to learn about dividends is in Chapter 29 of *Security Analysis* by Benjamin

Graham and David Dodd, published in 1934. Graham was a professor at Columbia University and wrote the book after being decimated in the 1929 stock market crash. This book is still a textbook used at Columbia and the first book any savvy pro will read if they have any thoughts of valuing securities. I wouldn't suggest you run out and get a copy unless you have problems sleeping at night. It's an outdated book by most standards, but for those truly obsessed with the markets, the ideas in this book have stood the test of time better than any other publication I have read.

Back then common stock was, well, common. Bonds and fixed-income securities were what the smart guys studied, and to a certain extent that has never changed. *Securities Analysis* was a breakthrough at the time and still is. It dissected the common stock that allowed a student of the market to not only simply analyze a company, but also to understand why and where *animal spirits*, greed, and fear live.

Dividends are not simply a method of profit transfer, but rather a place where investor psychology can be manipulated. Stocks are simple, but it is the human element that makes them fascinating to a market operator.

What did I learn from Graham about dividends? That the way we express them in the markets makes little sense. The idea about how companies should pay dividends was clear. During the time Graham was writing, the world had just seen the 1929 crash turn into the Great Depression. Graham knew that people at the time would rather have a bird in the hand than two in the bush. It wasn't until 1954 that the stock market got back to its 1929 levels. Meaning, if you owned a stock during that period, you wanted to get paid. The only way to do that was to make management dole out the profits. This was not always the most rational thing to do.

animal spirits   The mojo, baby. It's reality, nature, and the primal state of all things. When you graduate from college and you have to start paying your student loans, you start to feel the animal spirits. It's the thing that gets you up in the morning—gut instinct. It's not rational, it's right. Animal spirits describes the madness of crowds and the irrational behavior of people. It accurately explains why some people make money and some people are born losers. It's the difference between Hegel and Nietzsche. Nietzsche won.

What Graham set out to show readers was how to approach retained earnings from a business perspective, not to lure in investors with rich payouts. He thought each year shareholders should educate themselves on the business of the firm and make a decision of what would be the optimal way to use those profits. Shareholders would then use their education and business common sense to vote on the amount of profits to pay out in dividends. Okay, it's a great idea, but even Graham knew people were too lazy to do this. Furthermore, he argued that shareholders could see their best interests as stripping as much money from the company as possible. This wasn't just shortsighted greed. If a firm could make money each year, why not pay out all of the profits? This would in turn keep management lean and disciplined. It's a great idea, but when a firm gets strapped for cash it can go belly up. Also, some firms want to grow by reinvesting money, or need to reinvest to keep the profits coming. In the end, management is hired to make those decisions.

Unfortunately, all too often there is an adversarial relationship between those who run the companies and those who own the companies. Can you imagine the tense relationships back in the 1930s when the economy was blown up? Nobody was thrilled about anything. If people were to keep shares in companies, paying a consistent amount in dividends per share four times a year would probably convince them to stick around. Graham didn't think this was a good idea. First, in order to pay the same amount each quarter, you would have to hold back enough money to keep it up in the future. Nobody can beat a business cycle, and that means having extra cash around when profits are not as high. Cash just sits there, earning little interest in comparison to investing it. More importantly, cash sitting in the corporation's account is not as satisfying to a shareholder who wants it in his or her own bank account. To keep the savage beasts calm, you make them focus on the constant payout each quarter. You change the investors behavior from asking management "How have you been performing?" to "You just keep my dividend coming each quarter, because I have bills to pay."

The second problem with constant dividends is that investors will get used to them. Cutting a dividend, even today, can signal death. Think of the reaction when banks started cutting their dividends back in 2008. People thought it was the end of the world, which it almost was. Some firms suffered from pride, and in order to save face didn't cut the dividend, but also didn't have the profits to back it up. We all know what happens when you pay out more than you take in. Yes, Americans do this all the time; it's called credit card debt, and it catches up to you. By cutting the dividend too late, management can sink the ship.

Third, Graham didn't like the idea of constant dividend payouts because they were intellectually dishonest. He consistently talked about making businesslike decisions, and not trading on emotion. A constant dividend policy didn't address the needs of the company nor the shareholder long term. Both parties were fooling themselves.

Based on an interview conducted the year he died, Graham had changed his mind about a few key concepts. From his 60 years of experience in investing, no longer did he see the value in the deep analysis that his original work outlined. His observation was that too many Wall Street analysts existed with huge budgets for any edge to be had by the amateur investor. Furthermore, he admitted he was to a limited extent on the side of efficient markets, or essentially that you couldn't beat the markets. However, he still thought you could outperform if you looked at smaller companies that big firms were ignoring. I would not go out and start buying any small stock you can find, as even that market is picked over these days. Still, he explains that investors keep playing the game: "Common stocks have one important investment characteristic and one important speculative characteristic. Their investment value and average market price tend to increase ... [and] are subject to irrational and excessive price fluctuations in both directions, as the consequence of the ingrained tendency of most people to speculate or gamble."[1]

So, after 60 years of skin in the game, Graham observed that reinvestment of profits was the key to building wealth. While Wall Street was enjoying the sales pitch of dividends, by the time we got into the 1950s a new tale would have to be told.

Once World War II ended and G.I.s started to trickle out of colleges, our economy started a massive expansion that would last for the rest of the twentieth century. It's easy to look back and see that baby boomers were fueling the economy. Add the hindsight of increasing debt and leverage that consumers and corporations took on during the last 50 years and it is no wonder the U.S. economy was number one. Trouble is, when markets start to go into overdrive, people want to speculate. Coming out of decades of horrible stock returns stemming from the 1929 crash, the 1950s saw some potential for renewed growth. Wall Street needed to satisfy the greed, and selling a stable dividend would not do. During this time the idea of growth companies that paid no dividend became more popular. If you had a job and money to invest, why pay taxes on a dividend payout when the company could reinvest that money and increase the value, and hopefully the share price, of the firm? This was different than the widow and orphan mentality of the 1930s.

Growth Breaks Out

Reflecting this attitude was a reevaluation of the very notion of how corporations should handle their *capital structure.*

The decision to pay a dividend is important to the capital structure since it reduces the liquid assets of a firm. In 1958, Merton Miller and Franco Modigliani, then professors at Carnegie Mellon University, sat down to figure out the best way for corporations to build a capital structure. There were of course some important assumptions that only academics can get away with. For instance, they assumed in their theory that there were no taxes or bankruptcy costs and that markets would be rational and efficient. Well, that would never happen, but the Modigliani-Miller theorem would open the door for Wall Street to sell growth stocks to the public. The theory suggested that capital structure was irrelevant, meaning that the value of the firm was not determined by the mix between equity and debt. This was a big deal at the time, and years later would earn the two a Nobel Prize in Economics. A few years later they studied dividends in particular. Going along with the same idea that

capital structure   It's the blueprint of how a corporation organizes its finances. It's a reference to traders who are trying to find the best opportunity to profit from a corporation, whether it's a corporation's equity, debt, or assets. If you want to take control over a sovereign nation, the best way to do it is to take over its debt. If you want to take over a company today, the best way to do it is to buy all the stock. It's also a description for how a company seeks money from equity holders versus debt holders. If the company is strong, management will sell debt. If they're weak, they'll sell equity. A company that can borrow money (debt) is different than company that sells a piece of itself (equity). Debt is more confident than equity, since debt is an obligation that must be paid.

it didn't matter how a corporation structured the balance sheet, they had to come up with some reason why a firm would pay a dividend or not. They thought, "each corporation would tend to attract to itself a 'clientele' consisting of those preferring its particular pay-out ratio."[2]

Cults! After all of this groundbreaking financial thought, at the end of the day a corporation's dividend policy is all about attracting a certain clientele. Wall Street must have loved this news at the time, but knew this information already. People who want to feel safe and secure will ask the stockbroker to put them into some blue-chip dividend-paying stocks. Those that want action look for high-priced growth stocks, which most of the time have no dividend. For every investor there is a stock, and for every broker there is a commission. Now there would be no reason a go-go economy would leave behind the conservative crowd. Dividend buyers could continue to ask the wrong questions about how their dividends were doing, instead of questioning the reasoning behind it. Growth investors could focus on the rising stock price and ignore questions of valuation of balance sheets. In the end what was truly irrelevant was not the capital structure, but rather investors' desire to study that structure.

How does this affect the investment results? If it is just a preference by the clientele to go for dividends or growth, is there a clear winner? Ten years after Miller and Modigliani theorized about how the crowd acted, Fischer Black and Myron Scholes wrote "The Effects of Dividend Yield and Dividend Policy on Common Stock Prices and Returns."[3] They set out to look at the empirical evidence to put to rest the question of dividends or no dividends. After looking back at the performance of both groups of stocks, the conclusion was not what some had expected: "First, dividend yield does not have a consistent impact on expected return . . . second . . . expected return on the [higher yielding] portfolio, given its level of risk, will be lower than it might be with a better diversified portfolio."

Let me put this into plain English. A stock's performance wasn't determined by how much a corporation paid as a dividend, if it all. Sometimes higher dividend-paying stocks performed better, and other times they did not, compared to lower-paying stocks. There was not a clear pattern you could take to the bank. Their second point is critical. Trying to put together a high-yielding portfolio would get you a similar result to the broad market, but increase your risk. Why? You simply had a smaller, less diversified portfolio that

Philip Morris, the CIA, and Time Travel

It's 2010 and you work for the CIA. You've lived a good life and you're close to retirement. After going over your finances, you realize you don't have enough to retire. You've heard about how dividend-paying stocks are a good investment, so you decide to travel back in time to invest in them. (Since you work for the CIA, you're able to do this, obviously.) You head over to the CIA's astral projection room, inject yourself with a special serum which reminds you of LSD from the 1960s, and meet your younger self back in 1970.

It's New Year's Day, and your younger self is hungover. You tell your younger self to immediately sell your beloved 1968 Mustang, knowing you would need to sell it several years later after you have your first child. After paying $2,578 in 1968, your younger self sells the Mustang for $1,800. He takes the money and buys all of the shares of Philip Morris that he possibly can. On January 2nd, 1970, he calls his stockbroker Slick Jimmy and tells him to buy 50 shares. You give your younger self specific instructions to tell Slick Jimmy to borrow "on margin" the exact amount of dollars against the shares equal to the amount of the tax to pay on capital gains. This way he'll mail your younger self a check every quarter to pay tax on the dividends.

The Return

You pat yourself on the back, literally, and time travel forward to 2010. By the time you get back, your $1,800 investment should now be worth $1,629,900! But according to your statement, your account only has $1,241,705.19. What's going on here? But then you remember that for all those years you had to pay taxes on the dividends you received every quarter. Your broker also borrowed on margin (at the prime rate) the tax amount you had to pay every quarter. This means that in addition to tax, you had to pay borrowing costs. Between 1970 and 2010, you had to pay $388,194.81 in tax and borrowing costs. Without those taxes and borrowing costs, you would have earned 905.5 times your money. After taxes and borrowing costs, you only earned 689.8 times your money! Needless to say, at the end of the day, dividends significantly decreased your realized return, or the amount of money you took home after taxes and borrowing costs.

The Conclusion

This was a home run regardless of taking tax and borrowing costs into account. My point in making an outrageous example—including time travel—is to highlight the bogus results academics spew in mass-market finance books. It is easy to live in a fantasy world where you compound returns forever in order to show the eternal merits of stock investing. It is another thing to get a little closer to how an actual person could pull it off. My example, if not entertaining, is at least honest. This was still a lotto ticket trade. Rare is the fantasy from the halls of finance departments that includes the details necessary for the limited suspension of disbelief found in your typical Hollywood blockbuster.

in the end would have the same performance as a more diversified portfolio. Thus, you were wasting your time seeking dividend yield.

What's Next?

Should we give up on dividends? No way! In sideways markets, dividends pay us while we wait. Also, corporations should not hoard shareholders' money when profitable investments are scarce. Should Microsoft have billions in cash sitting around earning nothing? In 2004, the software gorilla had amassed more than $60 billion in cold hard cash. That year it paid out a special dividend of $32 billion to shareholders. Management didn't just wake up and pay the shareholders one day; they had been pressured for years to disgorge the money. Founder Bill Gates didn't need the money. He quickly announced his one-time payment of $3.3 billion would go to charity. This historic event underscores how a fast-growing company can hold on to your money for too long without sharing the wealth, which is what owning shares in a company is all about.

Wall Street changes with the seasons in order to keep the money rolling. Pitching people what they want to hear is fine if the product is solid. Is it really a crime to suggest Procter & Gamble to a person wanting a blue chip stock with a long history of paying a divided? Probably not, and if someone wants a hot stock there are plenty flashes in the pan to choose from. What you need to watch out for is when Wall Street takes your desire for safety—in this case, the perception of strength when a firm pays a dividend—and doesn't deliver. These days, the aftermath of the 2008 financial crisis is a breeding ground for deception.

I have been talking about banks for several years with a friend of mine over at the *Wall Street Journal.* His idea is simple and accurate: Banks are just leveraged plays on the economy. So, why would you want to have a bank increase dividends? Or more to the point, why would a bank seek to have a constant dividend strategy in the first place? Only a few years after the meltdown, several big banks that were bailed out started to raise their dividends. To recall, when the government bailed them out, one of the rules was ending dividend payments. Clearly, you can't take a trillion dollars from the government and keep paying shareholders profits that don't exist. It made sense that the banks wanted to reinstate paying a dividend, signaling to shareholders that the firms were doing better. Telling a shareholder that cash is better spent giving it back rather than reinvesting cyclical play   A way to describe an investment that is directly tied to the business cycle, which, contrary to what many people thought during the late 1990s, cannot be beat. The whole point of a business cycle is that there is a beginning, middle, and end. There's a point where it makes more money, it increases, and then it declines. There's a distinctive difference between the bottom and the top. If you want a dividend that's safe, I would not suggest a cyclical company. A secular play, conversely, is something that people need day in and day out, as opposed to cyclical companies who only do well during certain conditions.

it is a sign of strength. My issue is that the people who desire these types of stocks are not looking for a *cyclical play* on the economy. These aren't the big swinging speculators running their Individual Retirement Account (IRA) on "the E Trade." They are usually self-described dividend investors looking for a solid investment.

Wall Street, if it has done nothing else, has fooled millions of conservative investors. Well, up until about 2008, when they got a lesson in long-term delusions, mainly by thinking they had a solid winner in the banking sector. It's fine to be hoodwinked into opaque leveraged games the first time around, especially when the entire system to prevent this garbage was destroyed by Congress with the repeal of the Glass-Steagall Act in 1999. However, you know what they say, fool me twice. Or as I say, just give me a reason. Give me a reason to alert the bold and foolish lambs of the con that is about to take another turn.

The bottom line—banks reinstating dividends is designed to do one thing: Assure the public that the banks are fine. I agree that things at this point are improving, but this doesn't change the core issue. A new crop, including the original brood of the conservative dividend-seeking public, will once again engage the beast that wiped them out three years ago. Banks should pay out money when they can, but the whole idea of building up what appears to be a constant dividend policy for a type of business that can go south along with the economy will never make sense. If you are looking for dividends, look someplace else.

CHAPTER 12

The New Scam

Most of you may already think our representatives in Congress are out of their minds. Representatives in Congress create new laws without being able to know the unintended consequences. In this final chapter, let's look beyond Wall Street's desire to rig the investing game. As you will see over the following pages, there was a fatal error at the House of Representatives that opened up a new ball game. Let me give you some background on a change in the law that seeded this new game and how you can play it.

In 1999 a change was made which was possibly the worst mistake in financial history: the repeal of the Glass-Steagall Act of 1933. The most important part of our society is the banking system. Our entire way of life in America is based on our ability to print, borrow, and lend money. After the 1929 devastation, and more importantly the severe depression economy of the early 1930s, Congress established regulation that was intended to control speculation in the banking system. Also, it established the Federal Deposit Insurance Corporation (FDIC), which keeps us from freaking out and hiding money under our mattresses by guaranteeing deposits up to $250,000 per person. Of course, if you keep too much money in a bank and it goes under, you may be out of luck. Over the years, some customers who got stuck with a failed bank and held more than the amount FDIC insured got all of their money back, while others received pennies on the dollar.

How Did We Get Here?

Before the American Revolution, the British prohibited the colonists from printing their own currency. They did it anyway and just printed money with nothing backing it up. But it was the lack of banks that really caused problems. After the revolution, the United States formed its first bank on February 25, 1791. The goal was simple: Establish financial order and credit and resolve the issue of currency devaluation. Sounds like the very thing that almost went up in smoke during the 2008 crisis.

Why is the banking system so important to our money, 401(k)s, and the pursuit of happiness? Think about a child taking her birthday money to the bank. That child believes that when she takes her money to the bank, she is taking it to safety. Banks are safety; they promise that her money will be taken care of and that she can get her money back when she wants it. This idea was not always the case. It was not until the complete breakdown of ethics that came with the roaring 1920s that Congress finally separated banking and Wall Street. Before we can get to the tipping point in public outrage that led to the ultimate separation, we need to go back to a point when the financial system almost stopped.

If you ask most people on the street, they have no idea that there was a financial crisis in 1907, let alone what the long-term effects were. Stemming from the 1906 San Francisco earthquake, which started a long chain of instability involving everything from insurance claims on the disaster effecting U.K. insurance firms to the unrelated regulation of railroad rates, the stock market started to decline. Ultimately the market would lose 50 percent of its value from its peak in 1906. But the real issue that took the unstable market into pure panic was the rampant lending by banks and trusts (essentially commercial banks) to buy stocks. At the time there was no regulation on how a bank collateralized its debt. You could just buy stock and borrow against it. Problem was, if that stock dropped in value, the bank could go belly up. That is what happened in 1907.

In a nutshell, a guy named Otto Heinze thought he could manipulate the price of United Copper Company, owned by his family. This particular stunt was called a *corner*, meaning Otto wanted to buy up all of the shares and force anybody who was short the stock to panic and have to buy back shares. The dreaded short squeeze would enrich Otto and his buddies. It didn't work,

Otto failed miserably, and the shares of United Copper Company plummeted. This would not be a big deal if Otto had lost his own money, but his ties with banks around New York created a classic case of guilt by association. Anything Otto or his friends or family were involved in got hammered. Otto's brother owned a bank that used United Copper as collateral. That bank was toast. Then several major banks associated with these guys simply hit the rumor mill. Nobody had time to check the facts or look at the books, and who could blame them. Without a backstop like the FDIC, getting your cash out was the only way to protect yourself. News spread and a run on a few banks became a citywide scare.

Ultimately, J.P. Morgan, a financier who many people trusted back then, bailed out the system with the help of his rich buddies. It worked. He even bailed out the city of New York when the unstable market made it impossible for the city to sell bonds. Mind you this all happened within the same week. Once everything settled down, Americans started to wonder if this was the best we could do. Did we want to go through another crisis and have to rely on Wall Street fat cats to help us out when times are tough? Weren't they the same guys who created the problem in the first place? Yes. It was the banks themselves that lent the depositors money to the speculators, lost the money when the stocks purchased with the depositors' money went south, and then had to band together after depositors lost confidence. What a hassle!

On December 22, 1913, Woodrow Wilson signed the Federal Reserve Act. This Act of Congress created the Federal Reserve System, the central banking system of the United States of America, and grants legal authority to issue legal tender. A 12-member Federal Advisory Committee was created along with a single currency, the Federal Reserve Note. This was a big deal. Before the 1913 Act, *banks* issued currency. I know this sounds crazy today, but from 1863 to 1913 nationally chartered banks would issue currency based on the amount of bonds deposited with the U.S. Treasury, which then backed the bank notes. The U.S. Treasury formed the Office of the Comptroller of the Currency to examine banks assets and oversee the process. The new notes included new language that we take for granted today: "this note is legal tender for all debts, public and private." From this point on, regardless if the United States at different points in time backed these notes by gold, silver, or Treasuries, we would have currency that ultimately was the obligation of the

United States government, versus a bank that issued the currency. Our country's abilities to grow our economy, tax our citizens, and convince investors to buy our national debt are the only fundamental factors backing our dollars. When times are good, we tend not to think about it because those three items are strong.

The Panic of 1907 led to the creation of what we today call The Fed. People could rest at night a little better knowing that the government had the power to issue money the next time a run on a bank occurred. Did this solve the problem? We would find out after the crash of 1929 that the separation between banks and brokerage firms was the root of the damage. It would take until 1933 to address that issue. Compared to 1907, the 1930s were the end of the world. In my opinion, we got off easy in 2008.

The 1920s represented the start of our mass infatuation with stocks, fueled by an incredible economic boom that started after World War I. Since the Federal Reserve Act in 1913 created a lender of last resort, no longer would Americans have to rely on bankers to bail us out of a jam. Our own government would simply print the money and keep things going. However, what didn't change was the indistinguishable line between banks and brokerage firms. In practical terms, it meant banks were lending money to investors for stock purchases no differently than a brokerage firm would. Furthermore, without tight controls, you still had the potential of a domino effect if stock prices declined. Think of it this way. If your bank lends money to a brokerage firm and the brokerage firm lends money to a speculator, then a massive loss can spread back up that chain, just like in 1907.

The crash of 1929 was deeper in the systemic damage, and included a lot more people than a few speculators and brokerage firms. Remember, at the time our country had tremendous economic prosperity. Despite the fact that real estate prices had already started to fall a few years before the crash, investors continued to buy stocks on margin. Borrowing money to buy stocks created an artificial market that went up simply because people kept leveraging. Because of the lack of regulation at the time, too much money was being lent out to novice investors to keep fueling the bubble. To make matters worse, more money was being lent out to buy stock than all of the currency that existed in the United States. None of this was sustainable, but that didn't stop people in the 1920s any more than 70 years later when the same thing happened during the dot-com bust. What did change over those 70 years was the regulation that I think controlled the madness enough to prevent a total breakdown of society.

After multiple runs on too many banks, people lost confidence in the dollar even though it was backed up by gold. Unlike 1907, things didn't get better and a global depression followed in the years after the 1929 stock market crash. In order to restore confidence in the system, President Roosevelt signed into law The Banking Act of 1933 on June 16, 1933. We commonly refer to this as the Glass-Steagall Act. This came just six weeks after Roosevelt signed The Gold Confiscation Act. This act would be completely foreign to us today. Think about waking up one day to hear that all gold coins, gold bullion, and gold certificates were to be delivered to your nearest Federal Reserve Bank. Oh, and you had less than a month to do it. If you wanted to object you could face 10 years in jail or $10,000 in fines (Figure 12.1). Ironically, the Federal Reserve Notes and United States Notes not required to be surrendered still had "redeemable in gold" on them.

Keep in mind that at this point America was in a horrible predicament. Foreign investors, who up until this time had confidence that they could trade physical gold for U.S. dollars, lost confidence that the United States could continue to do it. And why not? The Bank of England gave up exchanging gold for sterling two years before. Since banking is based on trust and confidence, our country needed to enforce a separation from Wall Street. So the Glass-Steagall Act was passed and, for most of the twentieth century, Wall Street was the place for capitalism and speculation while banks were redesigned to create order and confidence in deposits. Clearly, Congress wanted to see if history would repeat itself when it decided to repeal the Act in 1999. Today, you can hardly tell banks and brokerages apart. But can you serve two masters?

History Repeats Itself

Most of us give little thought as to where our money goes when we deposit it at a bank. This leads to a philosophical question: Should we care where the money goes? We know now that a bank can leverage customer deposits by making loans for homes and vehicles. But if these loans are bad and default to the extent that the bank is no longer viable, the government either closes it or uses our tax dollars

POSTMASTER: PLEASE POST IN A CONSPICUOUS PLACE.—JAMES A. FARLEY, Postmaster General

UNDER EXECUTIVE ORDER OF THE PRESIDENT

Issued April 5, 1933

all persons are required to deliver

ON OR BEFORE MAY 1, 1933

all GOLD COIN, GOLD BULLION, AND GOLD CERTIFICATES now owned by them to a Federal Reserve Bank, branch or agency, or to any member bank of the Federal Reserve System.

Executive Order

FORBIDDING THE HOARDING OF GOLD COIN, GOLD BULLION AND GOLD CERTIFICATES.

By virtue of the authority vested in me by Section 5(b) of the Act of October 6, 1917, as amended by Section 2 of the Act of March 9, 1933, entitled "An Act to provide relief in the existing national emergency in banking, and for other purposes", in which amendatory Act Congress declared that a serious emergency exists, I, Franklin D. Roosevelt, President of the United States of America, do declare that said national emergency still continues to exist and pursuant to said section do hereby prohibit the hoarding of gold coin, gold bullion, and gold certificates within the continental United States by individuals, partnerships, associations and corporations and hereby prescribe the following regulations for carrying out the purposes of this order:

Section 1. For the purposes of this regulation, the term "hoarding" means the withdrawal and withholding of gold coin, gold bullion or gold certificates from the recognized and customary channels of trade. The term "person" means any individual, partnership, association or corporation.

Section 2. All persons are hereby required to deliver on or before May 1, 1933, to a Federal reserve bank or a branch or agency thereof or to any member bank of the Federal Reserve System all gold coin, gold bullion and gold certificates now owned by them or coming into their ownership on or before April 28, 1933, except the following:

(a) Such amount of gold as may be required for legitimate and customary use in industry, profession or art within a reasonable time, including gold prior to refining and stocks of gold in reasonable amounts for the usual trade requirements of owners mining and refining such gold.

(b) Gold coin and gold certificates in an amount not exceeding in the aggregate $100.00 belonging to any one person; and gold coins having a recognized special value to collectors of rare and unusual coins.

(c) Gold coin and bullion earmarked or held in trust for a recognized foreign government or foreign central bank or the Bank for International Settlements.

(d) Gold coin and bullion licensed for other proper transactions (not involving hoarding) including gold coin and bullion imported for reexport or held pending action on applications for export licenses.

Section 3. Until otherwise ordered any person becoming the owner of any gold coin, gold bullion, or gold certificates after April 28, 1933, shall, within three days after receipt thereof, deliver the same in the manner prescribed in Section 2; unless such gold coin, gold bullion or gold certificates are held for any of the purposes specified in paragraphs (a), (b) or (c) of Section 2; or unless such gold coin or gold bullion is held for purposes specified in paragraph (d) of Section 2 and the person holding it is, with respect to such gold coin or bullion, a licensee or applicant for license pending action thereon.

Section 4. Upon receipt of gold coin, gold bullion or gold certificates delivered to it in accordance with Sections 2 or 3, the Federal reserve bank or member bank will pay therefor an equivalent amount of any other form of coin or currency coined or issued under the laws of the United States.

Section 5. Member banks shall deliver all gold coin, gold bullion and gold certificates owned or received by them (other than as exempted under the provisions of Section 2) to the Federal reserve banks of their respective districts and receive credit or payment therefor.

Section 6. The Secretary of the Treasury, out of the sum made available to the President by Section 501 of the Act of March 9, 1933, will in all proper cases pay the reasonable costs of transportation of gold coin, gold bullion or gold certificates delivered to a member bank or Federal reserve bank in accordance with Sections 2, 3, or 5 hereof, including the cost of insurance, protection, and such other incidental costs as may be necessary, upon production of satisfactory evidence of such costs. Voucher forms for this purpose may be procured from Federal reserve banks.

Section 7. In cases where the delivery of gold coin, gold bullion or gold certificates by the owners thereof within the time set forth above will involve extraordinary hardship or difficulty, the Secretary of the Treasury may, in his discretion, extend the time within which such delivery must be made. Applications for such extensions must be made in writing under oath, addressed to the Secretary of the Treasury and filed with a Federal reserve bank. Each application must state the date to which the extension is desired, the amount and location of the gold coin, gold bullion and gold certificates in respect of which such application is made and the facts showing extension to be necessary to avoid extraordinary hardship or difficulty.

Section 8. The Secretary of the Treasury is hereby authorized and empowered to issue such further regulations as he may deem necessary to carry out the purposes of this order and to issue licenses thereunder, through such officers or agencies as he may designate, including licenses permitting the Federal reserve banks and member banks of the Federal Reserve System, in return for an equivalent amount of other coin, currency or credit, to deliver, earmark or hold in trust gold coin and bullion to or for persons showing the need for the same for any of the purposes specified in paragraphs (a), (c) and (d) of Section 2 of these regulations.

Section 9. Whoever willfully violates any provision of this Executive Order or of these regulations or of any rule, regulation or license issued thereunder may be fined not more than $10,000, or, if a natural person, may be imprisoned for not more than ten years, or both; and any officer, director, or agent of any corporation who knowingly participates in any such violation may be punished by a like fine, imprisonment, or both.

This order and these regulations may be modified or revoked at any time.

THE WHITE HOUSE
April 5, 1933.

FRANKLIN D ROOSEVELT

For Further Information Consult Your Local Bank

GOLD CERTIFICATES may be identified by the words "GOLD CERTIFICATE" appearing thereon. The serial number and the Treasury seal on the face of a GOLD CERTIFICATE are printed in YELLOW. Be careful not to confuse GOLD CERTIFICATES with other issues which are redeemable in gold but which are not GOLD CERTIFICATES. Federal Reserve Notes and United States Notes are "redeemable in gold" but are not "GOLD CERTIFICATES" and are not required to be surrendered

Special attention is directed to the exceptions allowed under Section 2 of the Executive Order

CRIMINAL PENALTIES FOR VIOLATION OF EXECUTIVE ORDER
$10,000 fine or 10 years imprisonment, or both, as provided in Section 9 of the order

W H Woodin
Secretary of the Treasury.

U.S. Government Printing Office: 1933 2-16064

Figure 12.1 Gold Confiscation Act

to bail out the bank. So as a society we should care what banks do with our money, especially if major government-sponsored bailouts irritate us. The problem is we have little practical control over how banks operate.

Add to this the hidden nature of a bank's book of assets that is all but invisible until bank examiners take a peek. Most people hadn't thought about this much because there are little signs at each teller's station saying that the FDIC will back your money. But 1980 started a 20-year campaign to deregulate and free up the restrictions on banks. It began with the Depository Institutions Deregulation and Monetary Control Act that allowed banks to merge, among other things. Two years later the Garn-St. Germain Depository Institutions Act deregulated savings and loans and gave birth to bank-sponsored adjustable rate mortgages. Remember that all of this was supposed to help people in an environment with double-digit inflation. Fast forward through the savings and loan crisis, a hot stock market, and years of profitable (for Wall Street) mergers of small banks across America and you had the perfect environment for yet more deregulation.

Since the early 1980s banks have been on a non-stop whine-a-thon about unfair limitations and the need to diversify into riskier securities. It seemed like a great idea. Let Wall Street, with all of its derivatives and risk-management systems, help banks control their risk. This would help the American people by providing more loans to more people with less risk to the system. What a concept. All you needed to do was break down the wall between banks and investment companies. Citigroup, the largest bank measured by assets back in 1999, could then create wildly successful mortgage-backed securities that only investment banks could make before. Profits would jump for shareholders, pay packages for executives that were tied to the increase in revenue would boom, and Federal Reserve Chairman Alan Greenspan would tell the public that the risk of system failure would be different this time. In May 2000, Greenspan said, "So long as we recognize the risks and insist on good risk-management systems . . . economic growth is, I suggest, enhanced by the kinds of financial innovation that technology and deregulation are now producing."[1]

Plus, with the government backing banks, it didn't matter if things blew up like they did in the 1920s or late 1980s with the savings and loan crisis. Banks were important and would have to be bailed out. "History teaches us that a sound banking system, willing and able to take deposits and extend credit, is a prerequisite for the long-term health of the national economy. Securities markets alone will never be able to substitute for the extensive and detailed knowledge that bankers—especially community bankers—bring to the intermediation process."[2] Part of the financial crisis was attributed to the local banker sending loans to Wall Street with no further responsibility. This made irrelevant the expertise that community bankers brought to the table. Was there anything we could do about it? As a consumer, did we have the opportunity to do business with an organization that was set up for us, by us, and had no other obligation to juice up profits? You choose who to do your banking with. At the end of this chapter we will take a look at an alternative, but for right now it is important to fully understand why the repeal was a disaster.

Of course, no one would exactly want to pitch the repeal of bank regulation with the argument that they would become too big to fail. So instead, banks told the government they were low-risk, would never do anything that would harm the system, and made the case that other countries do it, so why can't we? In addition they argued that it is not fair that investment banks can make mortgage-backed securities but banks can't. The late 1990s was all about deregulation as the key to economic success, and the stock market was not arguing the point. Investment banks would not complain since they would get fees on the merger and acquisition side. Senator Phil Gramm got the bill passed with the help of a slew of other delusional bureaucrats. This is the same Phil Gramm, king of deregulation, who gave us the Commodity Futures Modernization Act of 2000, which allowed Enron to blow up the energy markets. On top of that, it opened the door for credit default swaps to be excluded from regulation when transacted between sophisticated parties. Greenspan loved that bill when he told the U.S. Senate, "If our derivatives markets are to remain innovative and competitive internationally, they need the legal and regulatory certainty that only legislation can provide."[3] Bill Clinton signed on the dotted line. Citicorp merged with Travelers and everyone else got in the game. The Gramm-Leach-Bliley Act of 1999 essentially legalized mergers between banks, Wall Street, and insurance companies.

To my horror—I was working on Wall Street when it happened—the Glass-Steagall Act was repealed. Why did I care? It was a different culture; bankers were not part of our system. People see banks as safe and I knew at the time Wall Street was not and would never be a place for financial consistency. It had been only 10 years since the savings and loan industry blew up—didn't we learn anything from that? We needed checks and balances in order for my side of the street to keep on speculating. Now every bank was offering stocks and mutual funds to their depositors.

What a setup. Wall Street could now start selling garbage to gullible bankers on the savings and loan side. I was part of the Wall Street culture that saw banks as easy targets, buying all sorts of junk including bad investments. I had done a few trades with small banks. Usually it was through a connection with one of the officers. They just wanted bonds that fit a certain bond rating. Rarely did they shop around and never did they question the price. They just didn't seem to care since they were not highly paid and often didn't have skin in the game.

Besides, who would monitor all of this? Apparently, no one was watching despite the regulations on the brokerage and banking side. Just ask a bank trust officer and they will tell you about the hours of compliance work when you walk on both sides of the fence. Regulators were watching, but they didn't have the tools to keep up with the financial engineering and technology that Greenspan thought would usher in a new era of prosperity. This Internet speed of change allowed a few players like AIG and Lehman Brothers to get away with poor risk management, greed, and ultimately a system that would fail. It took almost eight years for things to go wrong. That is a pretty good run for an idea as bad a deregulating the one part of our society that needs regulation. I say it needs the regulation because a person's ability to get a loan for a house or a business line of credit isn't served if banks are dropping like flies. We saw this in real time during 2008. But how does this affect your money going forward?

Markets are tied to the long-term health of the economy. If we allow the lack of appropriate regulation of the banks to cause systemic damage to our economy, it will affect our society at its very foundation. Speculation, bubbles, and crashes are part of market cycles that can't be prevented. This is just human nature and we rig ourselves believing that we can control our emotions. However, when you damage the foundation itself, it can take years to recover. Japan is an excellent example of a country that has yet to come close to recovering from the 1980s. Their banking system was decimated, and their stock market with it. The very foundation of their culture was affected. Confidence in their financial system was shaken so badly that economic activity was and still is damaged.

America is a nation that lives and breathes finance. Manifest Destiny is alive in the very spirit of America and the financial markets drive us to make money, lots and lots of money. But you know what? It also makes us want to do things our own way. Every active investor has secrets that he hides from everyone. You think I'm lying? Look at David Swensen. He published a book a while ago with advice for investors. Then the financial crisis came, and it turned out that he had changed his own strategy and those who followed him without thinking ended up stuck in the mud. Regardless, the problem is we want to do things our own way so much that we don't listen when people are giving us good advice. I mean, I get it, we often think that we have conquered the past and we can make things work, but you know what? There is a reason Japan doesn't have a standing army, and Germans aren't allowed open signs of nationalism. It is time that Americans realize that we can't control our financial impulses without meaningful regulation or we are doomed to catastrophic failures and government bailouts.

What can we do about this? Simply understand what the question is and keep people on the topic. Financial reforms should be about keeping the system together, not punishing greedy Wall Street operators. Andrew Sorkin wrote a piece in 2010 titled "Punishing Citi, or Its Shareholders?"[4] In it Sorkin pointed out the hypocrisy of the Securities and Exchange Commission (SEC) for asking the corporation to pay a $75 million fine for misleading shareholders. But how were individual perpetrators dealt with? Sorkin highlighted the penalties for executives: "Mr. Crittenden paid $100,000 while Mr. Tildesley paid $80,000—was paltry compared with the $75 million that shareholders will shoulder. (To put this in perspective, Mr. Crittenden made about $32 million in total during 2007 and 2008, even as the company was foundering.)"

Wall Street needs to be kept in line, but sometimes in deterring bad behavior, shareholders and taxpayers (part of Citigroup was owned by the government at the time of the SEC penalty) pay the fine. Limiting its supply of capital, which is the fuel it needs to operate, can control Wall Street. Allowing banks into the mix provided a new supply of capital that put the average American in jeopardy—they have us over a barrel. Our government will have to bail them out or risk anarchy. Today we are making new laws to protect us from the changes that took place 10 years ago. Unfortunately, Congress is still in charge of writing them.

Further Down the Rabbit Hole

Now that you know my feelings on the separation between banks and brokerages, how has the game been stacked against you to create the new scam? Remember the time when cigarettes were advertised on TV? Not me, but if you are old enough you do. Camel commercials claimed that doctors smoke Camel cigarettes more than any other brand. Doctors want us to be healthy, right? So cigarettes must be good. Now think about when your brokerage firm started to offer checking accounts. I am not talking about check-writing privileges on a brokerage account, but a brokerage firm touting their new affiliated bank with FDIC insurance. After the barriers had been broken down, brokerages just needed a little technology to help the new scam take place.

Wouldn't it be great to integrate your brokerage, checking account, and credit card into one user interface? This would be another profit center and pull the customer into a more exclusive relationship. So brokerage firms started opening banks and providing tech-savvy web sites with the purpose of gaining more and more control of your assets. Around this time you may have gotten a call from your stockbroker announcing a credit card offer, and wouldn't you love to have the name of your broker on your credit card? The icing on the cake was the home mortgage, and more importantly the home equity line of credit (HELOC). This was no coincidence. Once Wall Street had the all-clear on the integration of banking products, it was just a matter of time before their management started to direct the behavior of front-line troops to sell the future.

Keep in mind that at this same time the brokerage industry was in a stage of price compression. This is a special term used by upper management of brokerage firms to describe the lower costs of trading and the erosion of profits due to people who want to pay less for services. Blame technology and worthless advice as equal partners in this crime against corporate profits. Brokerage firms, discount and full service, needed to find other ways of making money, and banking was just the trick.

When I was working at a prior firm, it started with a special incentive to open checking accounts. It wasn't that much, but came out to be around $25 paid to me every time someone opened a checking account. I was a little embarrassed about asking people to open a checking account; most likely they already had one at a traditional bank. However, management said every time you talked to someone you were to bring up the topic. A lot of clients said yes and the $25 paid for five to 10 minutes of my time to push the paperwork. No harm right? It wasn't like they were going to call me about it; the bank was a separate entity. So much so that my manager came in to explain we needed to place a special sign on every desk, including mine, that explained the separate entities. He put it in plain view, but off to the side. Who cared, the print was small and just said our bank was FDIC insured, but the brokerage side was not. These were checking accounts, not crazy investment schemes. Plus, some of the electronic bill-pay stuff was cool and not available from smaller local banks. The bank was paying very good interest in what was then a low-rate environment. This should have been the first clue. We all figured that it was the nature of the business structure. The only branch of the bank was in Reno, Nevada. Apparently you need to have at least one physical location, but nobody was ever expected to visit it.

Want to know something more outrageous? The firm sent out a letter to all of their clients that held individual retirement accounts (IRA) accounts that year. It was a friendly letter informing them that their money market fund, which was where excess cash in the brokerage accounts was held, would be changed over to the "Bank Sweep" feature. On the surface this sounded great. You would have FDIC insurance on what was before just a money market fund, not insured by anything but the assets in that fund. But what was really happening? The brokerage firm was switching tons of assets from the brokerage side to the banking side to boost the bank's deposits. It was nuts. Overnight, a bank that had nothing but a call center and a single location in Reno was now ready to start borrowing money from the Federal Reserve based on deposits that were created overnight with the click of a mouse. Each step was carefully crafted to quickly capitalize a bank in order to lend money on mortgages. Total loyalty would need to be enforced.

Step two was the credit cards. Hey, I got one myself. They were pushing the cards on anyone they could get to fill out the form or call into the credit call center. It didn't matter if you had a big or small account, or even if you had an account in the first place. The terms were better than other cards on the market. You could get points paid in cash, not plane tickets or overpriced goods, and I even got to book in the $25 incentive for my own card! Offering a credit card with better features than most was like a public service. Only a few people declined, but that was because they had a Southwest Airlines card and they could rack up points faster to visit the grandkids. I didn't mind the $25 bumps for doing next to nothing. This was the future my manager told me: Full integration to make life easier for clients. It seemed harmless and I was under no delusion the company would make more money this way. Plus, if people didn't want it, nobody pressed them. Who would hassle people for $25? That money was there so advisers didn't get irritated for pushing menial paperwork. All I knew was that clients were getting a lot more things in their wallet and in the mail that had the name of the firm on it.

Economists, along with Wall Street, knew at the time that Americans were using their homes as ATM machines. Did this particular act contribute to the expansion of credit and the overheating of the real estate market? It's hard to say, but I do know my old firm was making money off of credit and borrowing from home equity. Someone was going to get it, so why not keep it in house? This simple rationalization is the type of thing that rigs the game in the industry's favor. The desire for more market share of profits ignores the question of if a certain business line is good for consumers long term.

Then step three: Blue birds, lemonade, and a Porsche. Right as this stuff was getting easy, the end of my client list was approaching. I knew this since the company has sophisticated client management software (CRM) to track whether or not I had contacted each and every client about checking, a credit card, or whatever they wanted, all downloaded from corporate to my office computer. They can pull a string from two thousand miles away. By now the housing market was at a fever pitch, though it was going to tank soon. The bank had just announced it would go into the mortgage business. Of course, we were a wholesome operation, so none of this sub-prime toxic waste would be tolerated. Our services would be for people with high credit scores and of course, large balances on the brokerage side. This had limited appeal for most of my clients unless they were ready to move, and most were not. Refinancing was a topic of conversation, but at this point rates had already hit historic lows.

Why would any of my clients, most who owned their homes and had plenty of money, want to get a HELOC or mortgage from me all of a sudden? Simple. It was now my job and I got paid. Keep in mind I was not a licensed mortgage broker, but you didn't have to be. All I needed to do was get the client on the phone to the bank. Actually, it wasn't really the bank, but PHH Mortgage. They provide "Private Label Solutions" and according to their web site are the "mortgage engine behind many leading banks and financial institutions including Charles Schwab Bank, First Tennessee Bank, Merrill Lynch Credit Corporation, UMB."[5] Once, the person in the call center told me the Merrill Lynch mortgage room was next door. I plugged the referral number into the CRM, and once the deal closed, I was paid my money. We never called it a commission, but it is hard to call it anything else.

While I was able, over the years, to do a few primary mortgage referrals, most of the action was in HELOCs. This is basically a really big credit card that is secured by your house, but the interest can be tax deductible. I even got one myself, but can't remember if I got a sales incentive paid on my own HELOC like the credit card. It wasn't my top priority at the time, but then the contest began. One day an e-mail came into my inbox from corporate. Each of us had a few months to rack up as many mortgage products as possible, HELOCs included. Each region would add up the top producers. First prize was a Porsche Boxster. They even had a link where you could register what color combination you wanted. Talk about brainwashing! I decided on a dark gray with black interior. It was a two-year lease, but the fine print said they would pay for your insurance costs. Honestly, I had never seen anything like this at a firm with this reputation. Sure, at my original brokerage they paid for a BMW M3 (yes, young, dumb, and lots of speeding tickets), but that was the go-go 90s and I was making a bundle for the firm. We were also privately owned and didn't have to explain to shareholders why fast cars were being doled out to producers.

Needless to say I was starting to get a funny feeling that I was going back into the depths of madness. Euphoria, confusion, anger, and remorse all passed through my mind. While I wanted the car, I could see I was just a pawn, and not even for the industry I had signed up for. My hatred for the repeal of the Glass-Steagall Act intensified. But the system is rigged and so was I. The strings were pulled and my employer got what it wanted. I felt fine most of the time, and only felt like a bozo when it was clear that clients knew I was being put up to it. To be clear, I was selling credit to people who didn't need it. To be fair, it was a cheap way to borrow, and tax efficient. Add to this that my clients were responsible and knowledgeable but that wasn't the case for many Americans. Bad loans to people who couldn't afford them became a tragic consequence. While poor underwriting standards were not part of what was going on around me, the speed at which banking institutions could be created and start lending money was too fast for regulators to have much of a chance of finding the bad apples. There were simply too many fingers in the pie. For the machine to grow, more products have to be offered to a finite amount of people. When you reach the end of consumers who would normally qualify for loans, you can either pack up shop, slow down the lending process by laying off workers, or lower the standards and keep the party going.

Interest Rates and Yellow Trucks

In 1994 I saw firsthand how the first two options work. During a year off from college I worked at a mortgage company my father had founded years ago and later sold. I needed a job and he was able to pull some strings with the new owners. As soon as I started, interest rates started to climb for several months. My first day in January, I saw the daily list of loan applications received that was posted by the water cooler. I remember it was about 30 a day and was told this was about average. Then one day it came in at 20, then 10, and then plodded along in the single digits. When one day in March there were no loan applications, I knew I better figure out something to do for the rest of my year off of school or I would need to find a new job. If there was no paper to process, there was no paycheck. The company started to lay people off. This was the nature of the mortgage banking business and not a surprise to many.

Thinking about how I was supposed to earn my keep until December, I quickly made myself useful. By the end of the year my job was no longer processing paperwork, but driving a yellow moving truck to collect furniture and fixtures from branches around southern California that were shut down. Each week I would head out with a buddy who worked at the firm and we'd hit an office that had been shut down. He was dating the owner's daughter

(*Continued*)

at the time, so along with my father's connections we both had short-term job security. It was a creepy feeling going through desks and files, loading things up, and leaving the key with the landlord. It reminded me of those movies where the people are missing but their things are still there. I had a good time, listened to a lot of music played from an abandoned boom box from one of the offices, and bought beer with our travel funds. People's lives were changed and I got to see the remains of the day.

Getting fired because the housing market was slumping due to interest rates was not taken lightly. There were a few executives who truly believed that the company could keep running at full capacity forever, but an inexperienced college kid could see the writing on the wall. My father had seen ups and downs, so I had his perspective that things would recover. My buddy who went with me on the downsizing trips went back to college, as did I. Today he is a very successful mortgage broker in Southern California. He never left the business, and that year helped him understand how to survive during lean times. In the end the lesson learned was that a business cycle can't be beat, and when this company tried, it ended in disaster. You see, the reason why the firm was going down was the rapid expansion of offices the prior year. When things slowed, and they went from 60 to zero pretty fast, the owners didn't cut the staff quickly enough.

Fast forward to 2008, when essentially the same thing happened, only on a larger scale. What was different? The expansion had not only been occurring for several years, but the standards were being lowered too, so the mortgage people could keep making money. Loan officers were not given pink slips and let go, more were hired! Instead of the realization as in 1994 that there were simply not enough people who could put 5 percent down, we just started doing cash out loans for 125 percent of the already over-inflated value of houses. It was so far removed from the days I worked at the mortgage company that year that the news describing the housing crisis was simply unrecognizable from that awesome year driving around California in a yellow moving truck.

As a postscript, the credit card I still have from that company was sold this year to another firm. Clearly, my old place didn't want anything to do with credit cards in the end. What can we learn from this and how do we play it? Higher-than-market interest rates were a teaser to increase deposits. This allows the bank to borrow from the Fed in order to make profitable loans. This is how things got out of control and led to the real estate bubble. However, it is the system we use, so deal with it. The bank needed to seed the mortgage business, though they didn't tell you that at first. Take advantage of it! If a bank wants to borrow a lot of money to make big profits lending, they will pay you a higher rate. That is how the game is played. What do you care if they have a grand design and are not telling you?

Second, the credit card rocked. It had a great point system that allowed you to get cash back, but without all of the red tape and hurdles that other places have. Essentially, there was no bait and switch with this card versus most on the market. My old company was simply trying to get what is called *sticky clients*, meaning, the more stuff you buy from a firm, the less likely you are to leave them. However, nobody said you had to have an account with the company to get the card. Anybody could get the card; they just didn't advertise it to the general public with commercials involving Vikings.

Third, the HELOC was a great deal, especially since they didn't charge you a dime to apply for it, and the rates were very low since they screened only for top credit scores. The firm was simply trying to show Wall Street they were part of the great new era of fully integrated bank/brokerage/big brother business. The new world order will not have laggards! You must be with the herd at all times. My old firm simply wanted to sidestep stupid by avoiding bad credit risk. Your gain was their desire to impress Wall Street, but not risk too much doing it. Now, there is a difference between that and what Washington Mutual did, which was offer big savings rates right before they went belly up, so you have to do some homework. If your bank is in the news and the stock is in the tank, look someplace else.

In the end, I got paid, people got a decent product, and we all beat Wall Street at their own game. My old firm got analysts to say positive things about their banking growth. Yes, we can all win doing dumb things. That doesn't mean that we should take the risk. As a society we need to make choices that don't always benefit a corporation. There is a warm and fuzzy part of the banking system that I will end this book with. Even though the story of credit unions has a bad taste at the end, it provides some hope that all is not lost.

Credit Unions

Credit unions are not-for-profit cooperative financial institutions that offer similar services as a bank. U.S. credit unions are tax exempt, and limit membership to "groups having a common bond of occupation or association, or to groups within a well-defined neighborhood, community, or rural district."[6]

If we as a society are to make informed choices regarding how we interface with our banking system, understanding the options available is critical. Credit unions are all about people over profits. This is no joke. Back in 1934, the Federal Credit Union Act was passed in order to extend credit though nonprofit coops. Why should the banking system only be for profit-hungry vultures? According to the Credit Union National Association (CUNA), more than 87 million Americans use these warm and fuzzy institutions. And why not? Because of the not-for-profit nature, they should be able to pay a higher rate of interest on your savings accounts, and you pay lower rates of interest on your loans. By not having to turn a big profit, the savings are passed along to the members, which are made of the customers themselves. Unlike a bank, when you open an account, you become a member of the coop. Each depositor gets one vote, no matter how much money he or she holds at the credit union. This is extreme democracy.

Because of the more noble nature of the credit union, the government decided they don't have to pay federal income tax. Don't worry, all those tellers still pay payroll tax and any dividends passed along to the members are taxed. The savings add up, and bankers hate the competition despite being less than 10 percent of the market. Bankers can't stand even a tiny amount of competition when it comes to competing for your money. But is it fair that a credit union can avoid paying tax, thus creating an unfair competitive advantage over a traditional bank? Considering the tiny amount that credit unions take in market share, it doesn't seem to be hurting the public banking sector's profit margins.

Why don't more people use credit unions if they are so good for the world? Well, first we have to understand how they are good. Right off the bat they are set up to serve a particular group, not the general public. Not everyone has a credit union they can join, and they tend to serve savers of more modest means. Also, because credit unions don't have access to secondary sources of capital (i.e., raising money on Wall Street), they don't have the marketing budgets to advertise and lure in customers. In the end, they exist to serve people, not shareholders. By most measures, credit unions have made a positive impact on those that would be turned away by banks.

When Congress passed laws in 1977 to prevent lending discrimination, credit unions were exempt. Back then it was thought they were already serving the people that other banks saw as living on the wrong side of the tracks. We can track the actions of credit unions by a sample of data our country collects from the Home Mortgage Disclosure Act (HMDA). Established in 1975, this law requires financial institutions to disclose information about home loans. It is essentially a government watchdog group that monitors possible discrimination, among other things. HMDA data shows consistently over time credit unions approve more loans to low and moderate-income households than banks, not to mention minorities.[7] Are they just being generous? If by generous you mean giving loans to people that don't deserve them? Defaults from credit unions are about half that of banks, according to CUNA. If credit unions give loans to people they shouldn't, for some reason those people pay their bills on time. The bottom line is that banks assault credit unions with propaganda about unfair competition. The statistics show credit unions manage their capital better and serve average Americans who use them. If I were a banker I would hate credit unions too. But there are some issues with the utopian system that ends up rigging itself.

Credit unions have volunteer boards, and the members vote those people in. I am sure most are very well-meaning people that want to serve their community, but you don't have the top talent that big pay packages deliver. By their very nature, credit unions don't have the infrastructure of larger, private institutions. Automated teller machines (ATMs) are a great example of how big banks have limited the appeal of credit unions. For some consumers, having a branch in many locations and a national ATM network is simply more important that being part of a co-op. By having these operational disadvantages, which stem from the inability to create the profit needed to reinvest in long term projects like an ATM network, credit unions are not on the cutting edge of what consumers may want. Internet banking is more advanced on the for-profit side, though we should expect with technology that credit unions will quickly catch up.

By banding together, credit unions have been able to offer some of the services that big banks offer. For instance, some are part of a national system that allows members to use ATMs of different credit unions with no additional charges. But, what are some of the downsides of banding together? We got a dose of this bad news about a great community institution with the 2008 financial crisis. In order to achieve the economies of scale, credit unions pooled their money. Just like the banking industry, a few bad decisions

caused billions of losses in the same way that banks had their balance sheets damaged.

Corporate Credit Unions

Corporate credit unions are also known as the credit union's credit
union. They provide services to consumer credit unions including
short- and long-term investments, check clearing, money transfer
systems, and ATM networks. Without corporate credit unions, it
would be difficult to achieve size and scale to provide competitive
advantages to members. But this scale doesn't come without consolidation in the corporate credit union industry.

Since the 1980s there have been fewer and fewer of these back-
office players that act as the backbone to your local coop. Reading
the 2010 report from the Office of the Inspector General of the
National Credit Union Administration illuminates the problem
having too few organizations providing services to Main Street savers. The system of corporate credit unions was three-tiered. There
was one wholesale credit union that provided services to 26 corporate credit unions. Yes, you got that right. One firm, U.S. Central
Federal Credit Union, acted as the support system of the 26 corporate credit unions that in turn provided services to more than 7,600
local credit unions, or, as they say in the industry, natural person
credit unions. Then some very unnatural things started to happen.

In order to chase a higher yield on the money entrusted to them
by the natural person credit unions, U.S. Central and WesCorp (one
of the 26 corporate credit unions), invested heavily in risky sub-
prime mortgages that went south when the housing bubble burst.
Remember this is their main service, investing short- and long-term
investments of local credit unions. On March 20, 2009, the NCUA
placed both of them into conservatorship to save the entire credit
union system. In the end, five wholesale credit unions went down.
What was crazy about this system failure was the amount of mortgage-backed securities U.S. Central and WesCorp held. U.S. Central
held 49 percent and WesCorp a whopping 74 percent of their total
investments in subprime mortgages. Okay, you can tell me they were
lied to about the quality of the investments that were sold to them,
but nobody can argue that management neglected to manage risk.
You can't concentrate all of your money into one illiquid sector of
the market just because the rates are above normal. They are high

for a reason. Here is the classic rigged system where well-meaning people rig themselves. In order to keep up with the competition during the housing bubble, credit unions had to attract more money from depositors to make loans. They juiced up returns like banks and money market funds with questionable pools of residential mortgages. We know the rest of the story.

So, after the warm and fuzzy people-before-profits system was in place, it rigged itself out of billions of dollars and had to be bailed out just like the evil for-profit bankers. This doesn't mean you shouldn't support your local credit union if you have the opportunity. It does mean that we are still trapped by the larger institution of Wall Street no matter what our intentions are as consumers. We simply can't get away from the rigged game.

Afterword: Reading List

Usually reserved for the final thoughts of the author or an attempt to tie things together, I would rather move you forward after reading this book. Below are some readings that influenced me and you should consider reading. In order to make your life easy, I have provided a short description of the subject matter and who should read it. If you have time on your hands, I suggest you read them all.

- *The Money Game* **by Adam Smith:** My favorite Wall Street book of all time. This is the only book that I keep a copy of at both my home and my office. Simply stated, it's a 1960s rag on Wall Street and its culture. I find it most enjoyable because there's very little that clues the reader in to the fact that it was written 40 years ago. This is the first book you should read. Stop and get a copy now.
- *Security Analysis* **by Benjamin Graham and David Dodd:** While *The Intelligent Investor* is easier to follow and a more modern version of Graham's methodology, *Security Analysis* is where it all started for me. If you can't make it through this book and can't enjoy the history of it and the antiquity, don't tell me you're going to sit around and analyze companies, because you're not going to. If you're not mesmerized by the wealth of knowledge there, don't think about analyzing stocks on a fundamental basis. That being said, I think there is value in modern editions that have commentary to help the modern reader translate the more dated passages.
- *The Intelligent Investor* **by Benjamin Graham:** A watered-down version of *Security Analysis*, it's not a bad primer before reading the real thing, but no substitution for the original work.
- *Financial Analysts Journal,* **"A Conversation with Benjamin Graham" (1976):** This interview is a quick read on the Internet. Hear from the master himself months before he died what he

thought about his life's work. His answers will surprise you and will challenge how you view markets. For me it was a lesson in pragmatism.

- *Pit Bull* by **Martin "Buzzy" Schwartz:** A fairly accurate account of the personal toll that becoming a successful trader takes on a person. If you want to learn how to have a life-work balance, you have to learn from somebody who struggled with it for 20 years.

- *Reminiscences of a Stock Operator* by **Edwin Lefèvre:** This is not on my recommended reading list for you to buy a copy to put on your bookshelf. Read it for real. Make somebody give you a test on it. I have never seen a book purchased by so many and read by so few. Thank goodness it makes my life easier as a trader. If you want to understand the crowds, a word to the wise is sufficient.

- *Market Wizards* by **Jack Schwager***:* A wildly entertaining book about people who have made huge sums of money investing, speculating, or just plain guessing. A compendium of interviews with the most successful operators of the 1980s, *Market Wizards* gives you comfort that as long as you have passion and will, it doesn't matter how you invest or trade; you can find success. It is the ultimate motivational book.

- **Andrew Lo:** His views on risk budgeting are integral to how I manage money today going forward. "Reconciling Efficient Markets with Behavioral Finance: The Adaptive Markets Hypothesis" is one paper of his that you can read that is as close to English as possible. If you really want to get into it, go to Alpha Simplex group (www.alphasimplex.com) and read some of his papers.

Notes

Chapter 1

1. The World's Oldest Share. http://www.worldsoldestshare.com.
2. Scott, William R. *The Constitution and Finance of English, Scottish, and Irish Companies to 1720*. Vol. 1. Cambridge: Cambridge University Press, 1912.
3. Hobhouse, Henry. *Seeds of Change: Six Plants That Transformed Mankind*. New York: Shoemaker & Hoard, 2005.
4. Siegel, Jeremy J. *The Future for Investors: Why the Tried and True Triumph Over the Bold and New*. New York: Crown Business, 2005.

Chapter 2

1. Reider, Rob. "Volatility Forecasting I: GARCH Models." New York University. http://cims.nyu.edu/~almgren/timeseries/Vol_Forecast1.pdf.

Chapter 3

1. U.S. Securities and Exchange Commission. "Investment Advisers Act of 1940." http://www.sec.gov/rules/extra/ia1940.htm.
2. Ibid.
3. Ibid.
4. SEC Release Nos. 34-51523; IA-2376; File No. S7-25-99, April 12, 2005.

Chapter 4

1. Elstrom, Peter. "The Power Broker." *BusinessWeek*, May 15, 2000, 70–82.
2. PBS. "Worldcom - AT&T and the 92nd Street Y." http://www.pbs.org/wgbh/pages/frontline/shows/wallstreet/wcom/92memo.html.
3. Ibid.
4. U.S. Securities and Exchange Commission. "SEC Fact Sheet on Global Analyst Research Settlements." http://www.sec.gov/news/speech/factsheet.htm.
5. PBS. "NOW with Bill Moyers. Wall Street Email Trail Overview." http://www.pbs.org/now/politics/wallstreet.html.

Chapter 5

1. Charles Schwab. "About Schwab: CSIM Fact Sheet." http://charles schwabfoundation.com/about/facts/mutual-funds.html.
2. Charles Schwab. "Schwab Compensation." http://www.schwab.com/public/schwab/nn/compensation_advice/disclosures/schwab_compensation.
3. Pender, Kathleen. "Schwab raises fees on mutual funds." *San Francisco Chronicle*, May 8, 2003. http://articles.sfgate.com/2003-05-08/business/17489033_1_fund-supermarket-no-load-fund-shareholders.
4. Charles Schwab. "Schwab Compensation." http://www.schwab.com/public/schwab/nn/compensation_advice/disclosures/schwab_compensation.
5. Charles Schwab. "Learn More." http://www.schwab.com/public/schwab/research_strategies/mutual_funds/onesource_select_list/learn_more.html.

Chapter 6

1. U.S. Securities and Exchange Commission. "Findings Regarding the Market Events of May 6, 2010." http://www.sec.gov/news/studies/2010/marketevents-report.pdf.

Chapter 9

1. Stein, Ben. "Warren Buffett: Forget Gold, Buy Stocks." CNN Money. http://money.cnn.com/2010/10/18/pf/investing/buffett_ben_stein.fortune/.
2. Kennedy, Nathaniel. "Warren Buffett's Silver Lining." *Kiplinger's Personal Finance*, April 1998, 30.
3. Buffett, Warren E. "1997 Chairman's Letter." Berkshire Hathaway. http://www.berkshirehathaway.com/1997ar/1997.html.
4. Nones, Jon A. "Warren Buffett Sells the Family Silver." Resource Investor. http://www.resourceinvestor.com/News/2006/5/Pages/Warren-Buffett-Sells-the-Family-Silver.aspx.
5. "The Rip Van Winkle Caper." *The Twilight Zone*. CBS Television Studios. Los Angeles, CA: CBS, April 21, 1961.
6. *Gold Standard Act*. United States Statutes at Large, Vol. XXXI, 56th Congress, Session I. Washington: Government Printing Office (1901).
7. Green, Timothy. *Central Bank Gold Reserves: An Historical Perspective Since 1845*. (London: Centre for Public Policy Studies, World Gold Council, 1999).

Chapter 11

1. Graham, Benjamin. "A Conversation with Benjamin Graham." *Financial Analysts Journal* 32, no. 5 (1976): 20–23.
2. Miller, Marton H., and Franco Modigliani. "Dividend Policy, Growth, and the Valuation of Shares." *The Journal of Business* 34, no. 4 (1961): 411–433.
3. Black, Fischer, and Myron Scholes. "The Effects of Dividend Yield and Dividend Policy on Common Stock Prices and Returns." *Journal of Financial Economics* 1, no. 1 (1974): 1–22.

Chapter 12

1. Greenspan, Alan. "FRB: Speech, Greenspan—Banking evolution—May 4, 2000." The Federal Reserve Board. http://www.federalreserve.gov/boarddocs/speeches/2000/20000504.htm.
2. Greenspan, Alan. "FRB: Speech, Greenspan—Structural changes in the economy and financial markets—December 5, 2000." The Federal Reserve Board. http://www.federalreserve.gov/BoardDocs/Speeches/2000/20001205.htm.
3. Greenspan, Alan. "FRB: Testimony, Greenspan—S. 2697, the Commodity Futures Modernization Act of 2000—June 21, 2000." The Federal Reserve Board. http://www.federalreserve.gov/boarddocs/testimony/2000/20000621.htm.
4. Sorkin, Andrew R. "Punishing Citi, or Its Shareholders?." *New York Times*, August 3, 2010, p. B1.
5. PHHMortgage. "PHHMortgage:OurClients." http://www.phhmortgagesolutions.com/ourClients.html.
6. *Federal Credit Union Act*. U.S. Code Annotated. Title 12, sec. 1759 (1934).
7. U.S. Congress. Senate. Committee on Banking, Housing, and Urban Affairs. *The Effects of the Economic Crisis on Community Banks and Credit Unions in Rural Communities*. 111th Cong., 1st sess., July 8, 2009.

About the Author

LEE MUNSON CFP®, CFA is founder and chief investment officer of Portfolio, LLC, one of America's fastest growing advisory firms. A frequent commentator on CNBC, he also is quoted in numerous publications such as the *Wall Street Journal, Smart Money* magazine, and the *Kiplinger Report.* Lee's unique perspective on the markets is evident in the articles he writes for TheStreet.com and SeekingAlpha. He lives in Albuquerque, New Mexico with his wife and daughter.

Index